INVISIBLE
SELLING
MACHINE

5 Steps To Crafting an
Automated, Evergreen Email Campaign
That Literally Makes Sales While You Sleep

INVISIBLE
SELLING
MACHINE

RYAN DEISS

CEO AND FOUNDER OF DIGITALMARKETER.COM

Invisible Selling Machine

For information about this title or to order other books and/or electronic media, contact the publisher:

Digital Marketing Labs, LLC
4330 Gaines Ranch Loop
Suite 120
Austin, Texas, 78735

www.Digitalmarketer.com

support@Digitalmarketer.com

ISBN: 978-1-943046-00-3

Printed in the United States of America

Cover design: Britney Arkin

Interior design: Taylor Nelson

To Emily.

(Keep reading. You'll see why...) :)

Contents

Foreword

Leading a high-growth startup for over a decade now has taught me a great deal.

In particular, I've learned what works for successful small businesses. And not just based on our own success. You see, our purpose at Infusionsoft is to help small businesses succeed. It's the reason our company exists.

Small business success is elusive. As entrepreneurs, we start our businesses looking for freedom... the time, money and discretion to do what we want to do. But all too often the entrepreneurial dream is dashed to pieces by the crushing realities and difficulties of running a small business. There simply isn't enough time in the day to do everything we want to get done and there don't seem to be enough resources to make it all happen. Whether or not you figure out the best allocation of your precious time and limited resources, the to-do lists continue to grow, creditors keep calling, and the next payroll is just around the corner again.

The dark side of entrepreneurship is real. I have personal experience with it and have seen many others in its grip – financial hardship, strained family relationships, poor health, mental fatigue and emotional stress are common occurrences. Entrepreneurship can be really, really hard. Unfortunately, it defeats way too many small business owners. Perhaps you are experiencing the dark side of entrepreneurship as you read this. The good news is that there is hope. You can conquer the chaos of small business ownership. You can have the business you've always wanted and still have a life.

Over the past twelve years, I've personally met with, shaken hands with and spoken to thousands of entrepreneurs and business owners. During that same period, my team at Infusionsoft has literally talked with hundreds of thousands of people. Whether they sell a product or service, sell online or through a sales team, regardless of industry, location, or business model, all businesses have something in common. Without exception, every single business has the need to generate cash. As business owners, we know the central role of selling to keep our businesses alive.

Having worked with hundreds of thousands of small businesses at Infusionsoft, we've seen consistent patterns among those businesses that are successful and those that are not. Of all the possible variables that influence success, if I had to boil it down to the one thing that makes the most difference it would be having a systematic way of getting sales.

Another thing I've learned is that personalized, automatic follow-up works. Period. This truth is the reason I'm excited to see Ryan Deiss's work get into the hands of entrepreneurs and marketers everywhere. Ryan has mastered personalized, automatic follow-up. When correctly applied, the Invisible Selling method will enable you to engage with your prospects and customers in a powerful way to get more sales. When you create marketing campaigns that intelligently follow up with the right people at the right time based on who they are and the actions they are taking, it will be game changing for you and your business.

So, what's in the book? Let me give you a sneak preview. In Section 1, you'll get a sense for Ryan's expertise through a couple of personal stories, and you will also learn some interesting and important facts about email marketing. In Section 2, Ryan shares what he calls The 5 Phases of Invisible Selling. This isn't just a simple outline that leaves the reader with a bunch of 'How do I...?' questions. Specific examples along with explanatory comments are provided that will help you implement these ideas effectively. Finally, Section 3 is chock-full of insights and tips that Ryan has learned over the years to really make your Invisible Selling Machine hum, including how to create effective emails, lead magnets and landing pages. The content is so compelling you won't want to put the book down, and yet the nuggets are so many and so valuable that you'll want to refer back to it again and again.

I've known Ryan for a long time and have partnered with him and his company, Digital Marketer, over the years. Something we have in common is an absolute passion to help small businesses succeed, and I am thrilled that he is sharing his Invisible Selling method with entrepreneurs everywhere. Ryan is a natural when it comes to reaping the benefits of email marketing. Now you can unlock the power of personalized, automatic follow-up in your business by applying the proven methods Ryan shares in this book.

I love the value created by entrepreneurs like Ryan and like you! I encourage you to keep dreaming and keep working. You truly can have a successful business and still have the life you want. This book will help.

Happy reading and get ready to enjoy the benefits of personalized, automatic follow-up in your business!

Clate Mask

CEO, Infusionsoft

SECTION 1:

An Introduction to Invisible Selling

Chapter 1:

How To Create Money Out of Thin Air

I was 18 months into running my businesses when I first realized I possessed an almost mutant-like power.

I wasn't normal...and that was a good thing.

I had learned an incredible skill that became apparent when I invited a buddy of mine to play golf.

The year was 2006, and I was making good on a New Year's resolution. I would work Monday through Thursday—but Friday... Friday was golf day.

There was just one problem.

I only had one friend with the job flexibility to play golf on Friday and, after pressing him on why he could never play, he admitted that he couldn't afford a set of golf clubs.

"Really? That's why you won't play golf with me? If that's your only excuse, then I'll just buy you a set of clubs as long as you promise to leave Fridays open for golf."

My friend is a man.

And like all men, he is both proud and stupid. So needless to say, he not-so-politely declined my offer.

I protested, saying, "Dude, if you think I'm doing this for you...you're out of your mind. I want to play golf, and I don't want to do it alone. I'm doing this for purely selfish reasons...NOT out of the kindness of my heart."

My friend (again, being a complete jackass) still refused.

(Candidly, I'm sure I would have refused too.)

But I wasn't willing to drop it...

"Look, I'll make you a deal. I bet I can write a single email and raise the money for your stupid set of golf clubs in 60 minutes or less. I won't email anyone we know, and I won't mention anything about you or your complete and utter stupidity for turning down such a gracious gift."

"If I win, we get in my car, drive to the golf shop, and pick out a set of clubs. If I lose, drinks are on me. You'll still have your pride but at least you won't be thirsty. Do we have a deal?"

My friend, being the type of guy who turns down free golf clubs but NEVER a free drink, wisely accepted.

(AUTHOR'S NOTE: As I type this, I instantly feel dumber that this entire juvenile dialogue ever took place, but I promise I'm getting to a bigger point, so stick with me...)

We shook on it, and then immediately I sat down at my laptop and began typing. The plan was to run a special promotion to one of my email subscriber lists. Nothing special...just a "Flash Sale" offer for one of our older products that frankly hadn't sold particularly well.

Drafting the email took only a few minutes, because we run these types of marketing campaigns all the time. I scanned the email just to make sure there weren't any glaring spelling or grammatical errors, and that was it. The grunt work was over.

I clicked "Send" on the broadcast, and waited...

After a few minutes I logged into my shopping cart, clicked the "Refresh" button and presto...$17.

I refreshed again...$204.

I shot a grin at my buddy that would make the Cheshire Cat blush, and clicked the "Refresh" button again...

...$442

My friend was in awe, but I knew it was still early. Most of the emails hadn't been sent yet, and even less had been opened.

After all, less than 15 minutes had passed since the broadcast was sent.

I refreshed again...

...$663.

Momentum was building.

Feeling confident I said to my now awestruck friend, "You know you've already lost, right?"

He didn't respond.

So I waited...

...longer this time.

A full 10 minutes, which feels like an eternity, by the way, when sales are really rolling in.

I refreshed again...

...$1,309.

"Looks like you're getting irons AND a fancy new putter...let's go!"

This was my first experience deploying the "Invisible Selling Machine." My next experience would be a little more humbling to say the least...

Death and Taxes...and Email

My back was against the wall and I was scared.

I was in serious financial trouble.

My company had just finished a breakout year...our best ever by far. I felt unbeatable. Unfortunately, I didn't take into account that pesky little thing called taxes.

It was a Sunday evening, April 11th, when my phone rang. It was my accountant. The call started out well enough, "Hey, Ryan, you had a really great year last year."

Turns out it's not a good thing when your accountant congratulates you on a successful year. (FYI... It's also not a good thing when your accountant calls you at night, four days before your taxes are due.)

He proceeded to tell me that I owed a whopping $250,000 in taxes over and above what I had previously planned.

"Please tell me you made some quarterly payments I don't know about or that you have some cash squirreled away somewhere..."

I was silent.

I was in shock.

Spoiler alert: I didn't have the cash.

I was naïve. Heck, I'll say it...I was dumb. I hadn't paid a penny in quarterly taxes nor had I set anything aside to pay the IRS. Worse yet, what cash I had accumulated was reinvested back into the company the previous month.

I flat out didn't have the money.

(My fellow entrepreneurs and small business owners out there understand that there's a big difference between "making money" and "KEEPING money"...well, this is how I learned that lesson.)

So there I sat.

And, for the first time in my adult life, I cried. Right there in my living room, with my wife sitting at my side, I wept like a baby.

My Wife Can Beat Up Your Wife

I'm not asking you to feel sorry for me. This was 100% my fault, and let's not forget, the only reason I had a big tax bill is because I had just come off an incredible year. But that didn't change the fact that I was screwed.

As I sobbed in front of my wife (and this is why she is such an amazing woman) she said something I will never forget...

"I don't know why you're so upset. You'll figure it out. You always do."

And that was exactly what I needed to hear.

I made her a deal.

I asked if she would give me 24 hours to mope. One full day to feel sorry for myself. At 10:00 p.m. the next night I would get to work and dig myself out of this hole.

I spent a solid 24 hours moping around the house, wringing my hands at my own stupidity. But I knew what needed to happen—I had to generate a quarter of a million dollars in sales in roughly 72 hours to pay off the taxman.

So on April 12th at 10:00 p.m. sharp, I sat down at my computer and started typing emails. By this time I had several businesses, each with a list of email subscribers. More importantly, I had my Invisible Selling Machine.

At 4:00 a.m. on April 13th I pressed SEND on 6 emails and crawled into bed... exhausted.

I woke up the next morning not knowing what to expect, but when I logged into my shopping cart I was shocked to find that my efforts from the previous night had already generated $80,000 in sales. And that number continued to grow. On Thursday, April 15th, I wrote a check to the IRS for the full amount owed, plus a little extra to cover my first quarter profits. (I wasn't about to make THAT mistake again.)

For the second time in my life I had essentially created money out of thin air. I felt relief. More than that, though, I felt powerful...

A Shocking Experience of Power

I was never the cool kid in school. I didn't win Homecoming King, and I never hit a last-second shot to win a game.

I'm just a normal guy.

But that day I was different.

That was the day I realized I wasn't normal.

That was the day I realized that I have the power to create sales out of thin air...

...to create MONEY out of thin air.

I typed up an email, clicked "Send" and watched the sales roll in.

I felt powerful.

But the power wasn't mine.

Nothing in me had actually changed.

I wasn't smarter, taller or better looking.

I was still just me.

The power was in the system that I had stumbled upon. It was an Invisible Selling Machine, and it quite literally changed my life.

Since then I've honed my skills. I've learned sales automation and digital marketing best practices from the best—and formulated my own methods along the way.

And now I'm passing my methods onto you.

But be warned: Once you learn this system—once you experience the shear, unbridled joy of automated, invisible selling—you will no longer be "normal." You won't be ordinary.

There's an amazing feeling of power that comes from knowing you no longer have to worry about money. There's a tremendous sense of freedom when you have a machine that generates cash.

I don't say any of this to brag. I'm telling you this because I want you to have that feeling. I want to teach you these skills.

I truly believe it will change your life.

If you're ok with that, I invite you to keep reading...

Chapter 2:

But Will This Work For YOUR Business?

At this point you may be thinking, "Yeah, but does this apply to me and my business?"

"I'm a marketing executive with a Fortune 500 company..."

"I'm a local 'mom-and-pop' trying to compete with the 'Walmarts' of the world..."

"I'm a startup trying to break through the clutter and get noticed..."

"I own a private practice and I need more clients..."

"I'm a..."

...you get the idea.

This is important, but I'm only going to say it once so please, please, please pay attention to the next few lines in this book.

It doesn't matter if you have a big email list or a small one.

This isn't a B2B vs. B2C thing, either.

This system doesn't care if you're an online seller or a brick and mortar retail, nor does it care if you're a multi-billion-dollar enterprise or an "enterprise of one."

This system just flat out works.

It doesn't care what type of business you run. If you communicate with customers, clients, prospects and leads via email...it just flat out works.

I've been honing and testing the Invisible Selling Machine for nearly a decade, and I'm in a lot of "weird" markets including:

- Survival and preparedness blogs

- Industrial water filter manufacturing

- Do-it-yourself crafts and home improvement

- High-end men's clothing and accessories

- Investment newsletters

- Trade associations

- Small business lending

...just to name a few.

And it's not just me! Many business owners and marketing professionals (both mom-and-pops and large enterprises) have also put these methods to the test in the "real world." For example:

- Jean Cote from Success Dogs is a professional dog trainer. He's getting emails from disengaged subscribers that hadn't opened his email in months begging him to keep them on his list.

- Graham English is in the music market. He doubled his business TWICE and launched a #1 Amazon Best Seller book using the Invisible Selling Machine.

- Amy Jo Berman is a former casting director for HBO and a consultant to actors. She used the Invisible Selling Machine to increase webinar registrations, and brought in 40% new business.

- Mitchel van Duuren, a health and fitness expert from the Netherlands, brought in 3,000 new Euros using just one of the campaigns in the Invisible Selling Machine.

- Batman O'Brien (yep, that's his real name) has an acupuncture practice. He implemented one series from the Invisible Selling Machine and he's booked solid for months. It's impossible to get an appointment with him.

- Rich Thurman, owner of Shoe Thrill in Chandler, Arizona, wasn't sure if he could sell shoes with the Invisible Selling Machine. He used this system to turn $200 days into $4,000 days using the Gain, Logic, Fear campaign included in this book.

But that's just scratching the surface. I've trained and consulted with 100's of business owners, in every niche imaginable, to build an Invisible Selling Machine. Here's a handful of the markets we've applied this system to:

- Banking

- Veterinary services

- Motivational speaking

- IT Staffing

- Medical herbs

- Business coaching

- Web design

- Dating

- Water treatment/purification

- Photography

- Wine

- Mobile apps

- Small business consulting

- Health and fitness training
- Car sales
- Speed reading
- Healing rocks
- Luxury travel
- Music production
- Business consulting
- Art sales
- Retail shoe sales
- Fitness products
- Baby clothing
- Skin treatment
- Marriage counseling
- Private investigation

...I think you get the idea.

The point is, this works. If you want more sales, this works. And in the immortal words of Forrest Gump, "That's all I got to say about that."

Chapter 3:

One Problem, Two Mistakes and One Big, Fat LIE About Email Marketing

Email is an incredible selling medium, but there's one big, huge glaring problem. According to Fortune Magazine, the average person receives 147 emails per day. Yikes!

Remember the early days of email? People logged into their AOL accounts and smiled with excitement when they heard that familiar voice say:

"You've got mail!"

Today we're drowning in email with billions of messages hurdling through cyberspace on a daily basis. And it won't be letting up any time soon. According to a survey published by email service provider iContact, 56% of businesses plan to increase their email marketing activity next year.

There's a reason for the massive volume of emails businesses send each day: Email marketing works.

In fact, when you apply a solid process to it, email marketing works like a virtual salesman—driving sales day after day on autopilot. And if you really do it right, it can become an Invisible Selling Machine.

So, why isn't everyone doing it?

Most business owners I meet are paralyzed by the "small list" myth. They think they need an enormous list of subscribers to make email marketing work for their business.

Not true.

Ok, I'll admit it...

All other things being equal—a bigger list is better. But list size is certainly not the primary driver of email marketing success. I know lots of marketers with great big lists that don't make a dime, because at the end of the day, it's not the size of the list that matters...it's how you use it.

And the simple truth is that most companies don't know how to use their list. They don't have a process or a system, and that's the

primary reason business owners declare that email marketing doesn't work.

The fact is, if you do it wrong, email marketing doesn't work. That's why the rest of this book is dedicated to teaching you the right way to do email marketing—by building an Invisible Selling Machine.

The Great Big Lie

We've all heard this before...

"The money is IN the list."

Don't fall for it. This is a myth perpetuated by so-called experts peddling lead generation and list building services. We'll cover list building (this is actually the easy part) in this book, but only after you understand the Invisible Selling Machine process.

Make no mistake—simply having a list does not guarantee sales. There's only money to be made from a list if you have a "machine" in place to monetize the list once you have it.

We've acquired big businesses with big email lists that were utterly worthless. They had no process to extract money from that list.

This is what most marketers get wrong. They focus all their efforts on building email lists, and almost no effort on how they're going to make money from that list once they have it. So as backwards as it may seem, your first priority needs to be HOW you will make money from a prospect or lead. You must first have your process down, and then you can focus on how you will get more leads.

This is why you might think list building is difficult. This is why you might feel stuck. It's not your fault and you're certainly not alone, you've simply been taught to do things backwards.

Building an email list becomes simple when you understand the system I will outline in this book. The Invisible Selling Machine will give you an unfair advantage over 98% of your competition by deploying a simple, copy-and-paste "method" I discovered after hundreds of hours and thousands of dollars in trial and error of selling my own products and services.

These aren't sneaky, under-handed "black-hat" tricks and hacks and you won't be labeled a spammer. In fact, with this method you'll actually mail your list less frequently while making MORE money.

Two Crucial Errors

When most marketers get a lead, they make one of two catastrophic errors.

The first big mistake is that they fail to follow-up. It sounds crazy, but most of the business owners I know (even some of the really good ones) don't have a single follow-up campaign in place. They send emails to their list when they "feel like it."

Again, it sounds crazy, because what's the point of lead generation if you're not going to follow-up? The problem is most business owners simply don't know what to mail or how often they should mail.

Or they're scared. I can't tell you how many times I've heard business owners say, "If I email my list, people will unsubscribe." But if you're not going to send them email, what's the point of building the list in the first place? It's flawed logic.

In this book, you'll learn exactly how often you should email your list and the topics of those emails.

The second big mistake marketers make is sending the exact same email to everyone on their list. The fact is, not every subscriber on your list is created equal. Some are very interested in what you're selling. Others are somewhat interested and still others aren't interested in what you're selling at all. At least, not yet.

So should all these subscribers receive the exact same emails at the exact same time? Should they even receive the same number of emails?

Of course not!

Wouldn't you agree that if a subscriber shows interest in a particular product, service or topic that they should receive more emails than a less engaged subscriber? And wouldn't you think if you segmented your subscribers this way that your engaged subscribers would buy more?

And, if you laid off your less engaged subscribers, don't you think they'd stay on your list longer and maybe even buy something from you at a later date when they're ready to buy?

Absolutely!

And that's exactly what my "Machine" does and it does it on 100% autopilot. Now let's dive in and I'll show you exactly how it works...

ONE PROBLEM, TWO MISTAKES...

SECTION 2:

The 5 Phases of Invisible Selling

Chapter 4:

The 5 Phases Explained

Your alarm clocks buzzes that buzz you know so well...

Morning has arrived. A new day. It's time to wake up.

But you don't mind.

Today is going to be great.

And you know it's going to be great, because yesterday was great. Just like the day before that and the day before that. And the day before that.

You roll out of bed, put on a pot of coffee and walk into your home office. Your desk is small, but it doesn't need to be big.

There's no clutter. No files. Just room for your laptop and a cup of coffee.

You type up a quick email and press "Send" just as your coffee finishes roasting.

You get up from your desk, walk into your kitchen and pour a cup.

You pause, take a few quick sips and then walk back to your home office.

You log in to your CRM.

The sales are already rolling in.

You finish your coffee, and turn on the shower. You're ready to begin your day, but what are you going to do?

That's entirely up to you.

Because your work is finished.

Can you imagine a scenario more satisfying than that? Could it really be any better than to wake up, type out an email from your home office and watch the sales roll in each and every morning?

Actually...yes!

It's much more satisfying (and lucrative) to setup a SERIES of emails ONCE and watch sales roll in each and every morning on AUTOPILOT.

In this second scenario you don't even need the home office. Or the alarm clock. :)

We'll send over a million permission-based emails in over a dozen markets...today. And we'll do it again tomorrow. So I know a thing or two about getting ROI from email marketing and I'm going to share my system with you in this book.

But before I do...it deserves repeating that you don't need a big email list (or fancy software) to start seeing amazing results from email marketing. You simply need a plan.

We call that plan, "The Invisible Selling Machine."

Here's how it works...

Each email we send has one of five purposes:

> 1. **Indoctrinate** – Introduce new leads to you and your brand, and turn strangers into friends
>
> 2. **Engage** – Talk to your leads about what interests them and encourage them to buy a relevant product or service

3. **Ascend** – Welcome your new customers or clients and encourage them to upgrade their experience by purchasing from you again

4. **Segment** – Learn what they want to hear more about and what they might want to buy next

5. **Re-Engage/Win Back** – Bring them back when they've fallen out of touch or the relationship has gone cold

Each step builds upon the previous step, and works to seamlessly, effortlessly and invisibly transition strangers into friends, friends into customers, and customers into raving fans.

These are the 5 Phases of Email Marketing, and when executed properly it works something like this...

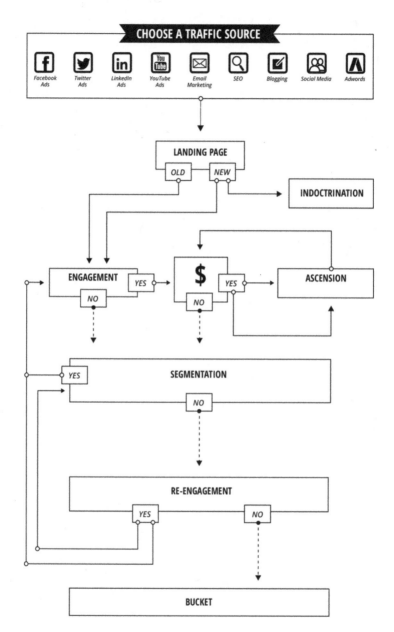

Want a larger, printable, full-color version of this process map? Just go to:
http://followupmachine.com/ultimate-email-gameplan
...and I'll give you that plus a video walkthrough where I break down each phase of
"The Machine" and how they work together to achieve automated, invisible selling.

Chances are your competitors aren't using all five phases. In fact, most businesses only deploy one or two at most, and this is an expensive mistake because each phase can produce a brand new revenue stream for your business.

But here's the big, big, BIGGIE your competitors don't understand (but you will). Think about it like this: A new prospect must be INDOCTRINATED before they'll engage with your message; must ENGAGE before they'll buy; must buy before they'll ASCEND; and once the process is over they'll need to be SEGMENTED based on interest before they become RE-ENGAGED and buy again.

In other words, it's a system, and if you leave out one little piece of the system, the entire machine falls apart. So to make this system work—to establish a true "Invisible Selling Machine"—you need to understand all 5 phases...AND how to move your prospects seamlessly from one phase to the next.

Fortunately, that's exactly what I'll be covering in this book!

To get started, let's discuss all five phases so you understand the role of each, and how they transition from one to the next.

Phase 1 – Indoctrination

Congratulations! You have a new lead. A prospect. A subscriber. Maybe they opted in to receive a special report or whitepaper. Maybe they signed up to receive your email newsletter, or maybe they called your office and left a message requesting more information or just dropped their business card into a fish bowl at a trade show.

Whatever the mechanism, the result is the same: You have a subscriber on your email list.

A potential customer has given you permission to contact them. This is a big deal!

Now what?

The first step is to teach your new prospect about you, your company and your brand. You need to indoctrinate them.

- Who are you?

- What do you stand for?

- Why are you different?

- What should they expect from you?

- How often?

- What should they do next?

Amy Jo Berman, a consultant to Hollywood actors (and practitioner of the Invisible Selling Machine process), describes the Indoctrination Series as, "Giving your email subscribers a digital hug."

It's a good analogy, because the Indoctrination Phase is about bonding with your audience at a time when they're most excited about you and your message: the days *immediately* following their initial subscription.

DailyWorth.com is a personal finance site primarily targeting women with an email list approaching 1 million subscribers. Here's what you receive after opting in...

```
Hi, and welcome to Daily Worth—the leading
financial media platform for women who want
more—more net worth, more self worth, and
ultimately, more joy. We're glad you're here
to embark on this exciting and fulfilling
journey together.

We love money. We use it to take care of our
families, our communities and ourselves. It
gives us power, freedom and balance. It lets
us pursue our passions, whatever they may be.

Ultimately, money touches every corner
of your life, and we're here to provide
```

the guidance and community to bring your
relationship with money to the next level, no
matter where you're starting.

Explore and enjoy,

- The Daily Worth Team

As simple as it may seem, this welcome email is still amazingly effective. You have been indoctrinated. Every sentence in the above email is designed to teach you what Daily Worth is about, so by the time you're finished reading it you know what they stand for and you've bought into their vision.

While I don't think this is the PERFECT Indoctrination email (we'll cover the *Perfect Welcome Email* later in the Invisible Selling Machine) this email from Daily Worth does a lot of things right. But they're not the only company who understands the importance of indoctrinating new subscribers....

TrunkClub.com is a clothing business that assigns men a personal stylist and ships clothing to you based on your personal taste.

The Trunk Club model is a bit hard to understand at first and Trunk Club knows that. So here's what they do to overcome that hurdle: They got me to opt in to a contest offer, and then immediately hit me with an Indoctrination email that teaches new leads about their business. The email begins by explaining the details of the contest I just entered and then hits me with this message intended to indoctrinate me to their process...

We'll announce the winner of [the contest] on
Monday, May 19th.

Until then, you probably have a few questions
about how Trunk Club works. To answer
those questions we put together this brief
video that guides you through the entire
experience.

Enjoy the video, and if you have additional
questions, just let us know.

Then, Trunk Club uses one of my favorite tricks to get clicks out of an email: They show an image of the video with the play button, and then link that image to the video on their website.

TIP: This is a great way to entice clicks because it appears that you can play the video right there in the email.

To answer those questions we put together this brief video that guides you through the entire experience.

Enjoy the video, and if you have additional questions, just let us know.

Even the mighty Apple knows they need to explain themselves to new prospects and customers. When you sign up for Apple's iCloud service you'll get this...

```
Now that you've set up iCloud on one device
you can set it up on your other devices using
the same Apple ID.
```

Followed by a list of benefits including...

```
Access your music, movies, apps and books
on your iPhone, iPad, iPod touch, and Mac –
wirelessly without syncing.
```

And, as you might expect, this email links to a "Learn More" page that explains all of these benefits of using iCloud. In short, they're teaching me the process—because I'm new and I'm excited about it.

You might find that a single Indoctrination email is sufficient... but more likely it will be more effective sent as a series.

Fizzle.co sells a membership site with training courses and other content on running a small business. Here's the second email in a series intended to indoctrinate new subscribers into the "Fizzle Way"...

> I noticed you signed up for Fizzle. Welcome to the group!
>
> If you have a second, I'd love to know:
>
> Why did you sign up for Fizzle?
>
> What do you hope Fizzle can help you achieve?
>
> Thanks for joining us; we're really glad to have you.
>
> ~ Corbett
>
> P.S. The door is always open. If you have any questions or feedback, email anytime.
>
> Oh, and here's a bonus question if you're so inclined to answer: What do you hope to contribute to the Fizzle community?

Notice the email is signed by the founder (Corbett Barr), and he's asking you to engage with the email by replying back. This is important and we'll talk more about why in a second.

Once you've indoctrinated your prospect... you can move them into an Engagement Series.

Phase 2 – Engagement

The role of an Engagement email is simple: To convert prospects into customers. In other words, Engagement emails make offers and ask for the order.

In this example, HubSpot is attempting to engage me in their partner program. This email was triggered when I downloaded a free report and indicated that my business is an agency...

> I noticed you recently expressed an interest in HubSpot and some of our content.
>
> Through our partner program for firms like yours, we've helped many of our partners expand and grow their businesses with longer and larger monthly service retainers.
>
> I'd recommend starting a trial at Hubspot.com to start the process and begin exploring.
>
> Our Partner Program has helped marketing agencies with the following areas...
>
> *(They then proceed to list the benefits of this offer and close with...)*
>
> Are you looking for help with any of the above? If so, let me know if you'd like to chat over the phone to learn more.
>
> ~Chris

Again, this email is signed by a real person—not the company—which increases engagement in the email. It also encourages me to respond, which again increases liking and engagement, and ideally (from HubSpot's perspective) causes me to take a trial of their software.

We're going to cover the Engagement Series in greater depth in this book, but here's one more example just to make sure this concept is sinking in.

The cart abandonment series is a staple Engagement email for smart online retailers.

Lowe's knows the drill.

After adding some patio chairs to my shopping cart and abandoning the cart, I got an email with the subject line, "Don't Let Your Shopping Cart Disappear."

Using email to pull prospects that were SO CLOSE to converting back into the shopping cart is a smart use of the Invisible Selling Machine.

Your business can see big gains by simply plugging in an Engagement Series, and in a later chapter I'll show you a copy-and-paste-simple way to do just that.

Once you've engaged your audience... it's time for an Ascension Series.

Phase 3 – Ascension

This is where the big money is made, so listen up...

For every offer you make to your audience, there is some percentage of buyers that would buy more. And that's why every buyer you acquire through an Engagement email series should receive an Ascension Series email immediately after their initial purchase.

Here's an example so you can see what I mean...

This Ascension offer from StudioPress.com was sent to customers that had previously purchased one of their WordPress themes...

```
Hey gang,

I'm going to keep this short and very sweet
- a simple reminder that - because you are
our awesome StudioPress customers - you
get 25% off anything your purchase over at
StudioPress.com.

No catch. No coupons. No complications.

Just a full 25% off when you log in...

[LINK TO LOG IN PAGE]

... and get yourself a brand new theme.

Or, how about you go ahead and cure all of
your design headaches once and for all by
purchasing the Pro Plus All-Theme Package?

Get anything you want and we'll get you that
25% off.
```

While this email would have been more effective if it were directed at a single person as opposed to a group of people, the overall strategy is sound. The folks over at StudioPress know I buy WordPress themes, so why not offer to sell me more? The fact that I purchased one theme doesn't make me less likely to purchase another. The opposite is true! The fact that I purchased one theme actually makes me MORE LIKELY to purchase again. I'm a theme buyer! It's not a subjective guess or hope...it's an objective fact.

And you can use these objective facts to your advantage to turn buyers into multi-buyers...but you have to do it the right way or you will annoy your best customers. (Fortunately, I'm going to show you how to do it the right way in a later chapter.) But first, let's discuss a few more examples...

The entry-level offer over at MarketingProfs.com gets you access to their free content, but they are quick to move me into an Ascension Series to upgrade me to Marketing Profs Pro.

This Ascension email is interesting because it uses a story about a Marketing Consultant name Sharon, and includes a picture of Sharon along with this copy...

PRO propels your performance

Sharon credits her PRO membership for helping her improve her writing skills, find her voice, and trust her marketing instincts. She takes advantage of her exclusive PRO access to seminars (both live and on-demand), how-to guides, Take 10 video tutorials, and being the social butterfly she is; she's found that she fits right into our Pro community.

Notice how Marketing Profs uses the story to convince me to ascend. Heck, if Sharon can do it, SO CAN I!

The non-profit charity: water follows-up with contributors to show them the impact their donation is having—and closes with a call to action to ascend to start their own fundraising campaign...

START A FUNDRAISING CAMPAIGN OF YOUR OWN!

Now that you've seen proof of your donation, why not do even more? Start a fundraising campaign. We'll track every donation you get and show you proof. 100% of every dollar directly funds water project costs in the field.

So...what do you do when customers and prospects say "NO" to the Engagement or Ascension Series you send them?

Simple... you change the message until they respond, which exactly the role of the Segmentation Phase...

Phase 4 – Segmentation

The goal of the Segmentation Series is to get your prospect to "raise their hand" and show interest in a particular topic by either opening, clicking or opting in to a relevant offer. And when they take this action (i.e. when the Segmentation Series has done its job) the prospect will then be placed into an appropriate Engagement Series.

Notice how Joe Polish from *Piranha Marketing* uses questions to determine my interest in his Genius Network Event...

Joe Polish wanted me to get this to you right away...

[LINK TO A VIDEO]

Successful Entrepreneurs like you are 100% committed to the value you create.

But... does creating that value sometimes get in the way of your health, or in the way of relationships that are most important to you?

We just got official confirmation from Arianna Huffington that she will be at the upcoming Genius Network Annual Event...

The email goes on to explain the value of the event. But what's interesting is the follow-up email I receive if I click on the links in this email. With just a single click, I have been segmented...

> Thanks so much for checking out the Genius Network Annual Event Preview package along with the bonus videos that Joe's making available to help you get more clarity and capabilities to grow your business.

In fact, by segmenting myself (clicking on a link in the first email to learn more) I received a number of follow-up emails in an Engagement Series about this offer.

Here's how Marriot is handling segmentation: Clicking on any of the offers below displays interest and segments the list.

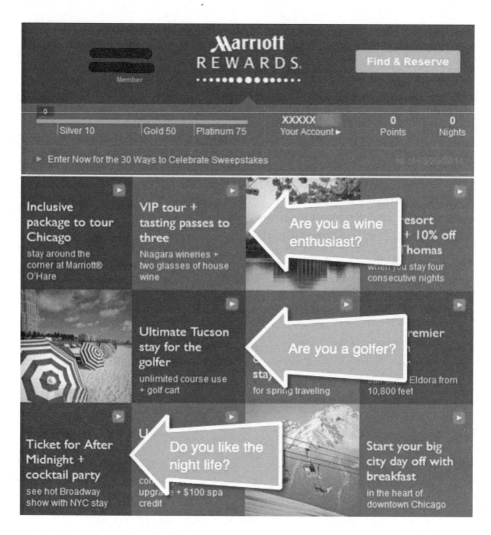

Are you seeing the power of Segmentation and how it feeds prospects back into your Engagement and Ascension Series? Sending a single Segmentation email to your list can set off a chain reaction of sales.

Ok... now let's take a high-level look at the simplest (and often the most impactful) stage of email marketing...

Phase 5 – Re-Engagement

So what happens when customers and prospects stop opening and clicking on your email?

If your answer is NOTHING—you're leaving big money on the table.

Setting up a Re-Engagement and Win Back Series is the lowest of low-hanging fruit. If they were interested once, chances are they'll be interested again. You just have to give them something that will re-energize and re-engage their interest in what you have to say.

But that's just half the benefit...

Leaving disengaged emails on your list does tremendous damage to your email deliverability, so by re-engaging subscribers that have strayed from the pack, you'll also avoid the Spam folder. (More on this later...)

Notice how LinkedIn reinforces the value of their LinkedIn Today emails with this re-engagement email and threatens to take it away if no action is taken...

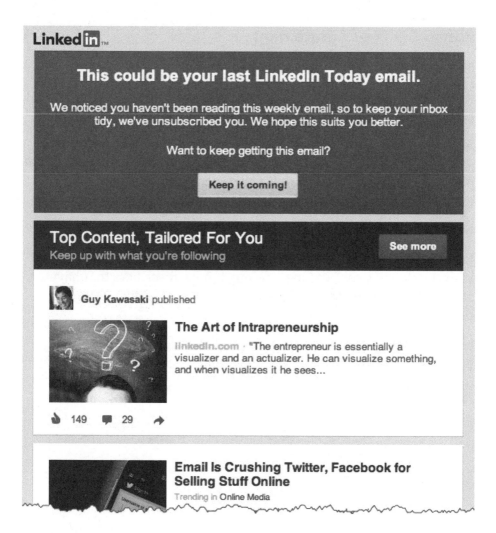

HealthCare.gov had their work cut out for them after thousands of people created accounts but couldn't complete their registration. So they sent emails with this copy to re-engage those that started the process but hadn't returned...

> If you were trying to enroll for 2014
> coverage by the March 31st enrollment
> deadline and experienced system delays caused
> by heavy traffic, maintenance periods, or
> other special situations that prevented you

```
from finishing the process on time, we may
still be able to help you get covered.
```

This email copy was followed by a button with the call to action, "FINISH ENROLLING."

At Pinkberry, they use a loyalty rewards card to track defecting customers and make a win back offer when customers haven't visited in a while...

Netflix makes a win back offer to customers that cancel their subscription with this copy...

```
Come back today and get another FREE trial

Dear Ryan,

We'd like to offer you another free trial!
We're always adding more TV shows & movies
for you to enjoy instantly. Come back to
Netflix today and check out what's new - for
FREE.
```

The email then states the benefits of a Netflix subscription and ends with a button with the call to action, "Start Your Free Trial."

How could you use email to reengage and win back customers and prospects? Don't worry if you can't answer that question just yet, because more ideas will follow a little later in this book.

Enough Overview...Let's Get Started!

So how do you get started?

How do you build and launch your own Invisible Selling Machine?

It starts with understanding that the 5 stages of email marketing exist. After that, it's a matter of determining where you can make the most impact on your business.

- Can an Indoctrination campaign produce more engaged prospects that are eagerly awaiting your next email?

- Should you build an Engagement Series to revive an old product or service?

- Could you squeeze more ROI from your customers with an Ascension Series?

- Can you make relevant, high-converting offers to your list by sending a Segmentation email?

- Would a Re-Engagement and Win Back Series bring 5, 10 or 15% of your list back to buy?

The answer is YES on all accounts, but where you begin is up to you.

The bulk of this book is focused on taking deep dives on the 5 stages of automated email marketing and we begin with the critical early days of your relationship with a new lead.

Chapter 5:

Phase 1 – Indoctrination

What's the first thing you do with a new lead?

First, understand that they are more excited to hear from you at this moment than they will ever be. Play your cards right, and you'll be a friend forever. Squander it, and you'll be seen as a spammer in under a week. What will you do with this precious time? How will you ensure that your new subscriber will look forward to receiving your emails?

The answer: Indoctrination.

Now is the time to:

- Introduce yourself/your company

- Set expectations for what they will receive

- Restate the benefits of being a subscriber/lead

- Get them to make micro-commitments

- Open a "curiosity loop" (so they wait on pins and needles for your next message).

If you craft this first Indoctrination email (called the Welcome Email) properly, you'll be much more likely to convert this lead to a customer. More importantly, you'll turn a stranger into a friend of you and your brand.

Let's take a look at each element of the welcome email in detail...

Introductions

Your Welcome Email (in most cases) should come from a real human... not the company. The CEO (or other face of the company) is a good person to put in the FROM line on an Indoctrination email.

It's as simple as stating...

```
Hi, My name is Ryan Deiss and I'm the founder of
Digital Marketer. I wanted to take a second to
say hello and welcome you to the family.
```

Set Expectations

Tell them exactly what to expect from you, when and how often. Say something like...

```
Here's what you can expect from us...
```

Then, simply list everything they will begin receiving from you via email (and otherwise) now that they are a subscriber.

This includes letting them know, in a subtle way, that you will be sending promotional email.

Restate Benefits

While you're telling them what they should expect, restate the benefits of these communications. Something like this will do the trick...

```
I know this is going to be an absolute game
changer for you because...
```

Don't expect your new subscriber to connect the dots. Hit them over the head with benefits and take advantage of their attention to build excitement and anticipation for future communications.

Ask Them to Whitelist You (and More)

In future emails you'll be asking your subscriber to do things such as read a blog post, download a white paper or purchase an offer. An Indoctrination email is the time to start training your new subscribers to make small commitments.

The first micro-commitment is to ask them to "whitelist" your email address to ensure safe delivery of your email to their inbox. Remember, they just opted in to your list so they're excited to be receiving email from you—take advantage of that.

Create and link to a page on your website that gives clear whitelisting instructions (see ours at: http://www.digitalmarketer.com/email-whitelisting/).

Let them know that they run the risk of not receiving your emails if they don't whitelist you.

Second, ask them to connect with you outside of email. This is where you can increase engagement with your new subscriber on social media. We'll talk more about why engagement is so critical to today's email marketer in a second. (Hint: We aren't talking about fluffy, hippy marketer engagement metrics here.)

Say something like...

```
Take two seconds and join us on [FACEBOOK,
TWITTER, YOU TUBE, LINKED IN].
```

Opening Curiosity Loops

Do you know why your favorite TV drama ends every episode with a cliffhanger?

Cliffhangers create tension, and tension creates attention.

In fact, you should probably say that 5 times fast...

Tension creates attention...

Tension creates attention...

Tension creates attention...

Tension creates attention...

Tension creates attention...

The human brain craves conclusions, which is why the best emails leave your subscriber on the edge of their seat—anxiously awaiting your next email.

This cliffhanger effect is also called "opening a loop," and your Indoctrination email should contain at least one. In fact, open loops are something we'll come back to in all phases of the Invisible Selling Machine, because they just flat out work.

Here's an example of an open loop you can deploy in your welcome messages...

```
As an added bonus for subscribing, I'm going
to be sending you my best [white paper/blog
posts/case studies/tools, etc.] It's about
[INSERT SOMETHING YOU KNOW YOUR SUBSCRIBER
ACTUALLY WANTS]. Be on the lookout for an
email from me tomorrow.
```

OR...

```
Do you know the #1 reason why [INSERT A
RIDDLE/REASON WHY/ETC]? I bet it's not the
reason you think. I'll give you the answer
tomorrow but for now...
```

In both examples, the subscriber is told that they're going to receive something incredible...something they actually want. Unfortunately, they're going to have to wait for it. And that's exactly what we want, because when that second email arrives, you better believe it's going to get opened and consumed.

But "open loops" are just one method for increasing engagement and intimacy during the Indoctrination Phase. A second strategy you can deploy is known as "bouncing"...

"Bounce" Them Around

I saved this for last, because it may be the most important purpose of your Indoctrination email. The primary metric used to determine whether your future emails will make it to the inbox or the SPAM box is engagement. In other words, when your subscribers take actions like...

- Open your email...

- Click on a link in your email...

- Favorite/Star your email, or...

- Reply to your email...

... they are much more likely to continue receiving your emails.

Why? Because the big Internet services providers (ISPs), services like Gmail, Yahoo Mail and Hotmail, all look at these factors to determine if your emails are legitimate or if they are SPAM. If your emails are getting opened, clicked and replied to on a regular basis, the ISPs deem your messages "worthy" (meaning they hit the primary inbox as opposed to the Spam folder). If, however, your emails have limited engagement, you can kiss the inbox good-bye.

Many of the elements of this Indoctrination email are intended to increase these engaging actions. For example, asking your new subscribers to "whitelist" your emails increases deliverability and is an engagement trigger. In fact, just the act of them clicking on your "whitelisting instructions" link increases clicks-through rates, which is a measure of engagement.

Also, clicks on social media links increase click-through rates of the emails, which is a sign of engagement. More importantly, when your subscribers follow your brand on Facebook and Twitter, this increases the chance that they'll open your emails in the future. And increased open rates increase...you guessed it...ENGAGEMENT!

That's why the perfect welcome mail not only indoctrinates your new subscribers to your brand and message, it also gets them to take specific actions that will improve your deliverability and ensure your emails hit the primary inbox, and not some secondary folder or "Spam" box.

Also, when your new subscriber "bounces" from your email...to your Facebook page...to your Twitter page...to your whitelisting page... etc....the mere act of "movement" increases intimacy and makes them more likely to like you and engage with your future email.

And none of this is theory. It's a fact of human relationships...

The concept of "bouncing" actually comes from the Pick-Up Artist space—you know those sleazy guys that go from bar to bar picking up woman? (AUTHOR'S NOTE: I am a happily married man, so while I am not a student of "pick-up artists" for the sake of picking up women, I am a student of psychology, which is how I came across this research. I just wanted to clarify that in case my wonderful wife happens upon this book and actually reads it to this point.) :)

The goal of the pick-up artist is to increase intimacy with a woman as quickly as possible, because after all, what well-meaning woman is going to go home with a man she just met? That's where "bouncing" comes into play. It's a simple technique, but devilishly effective. All the pick-up artist has to do is ask the lady to move from one area of the club or bar to another area, multiple times.

For example:

They might meet a girl on the dance floor...

...and then suggest that they walk over to the bar...

...and then encourage them to walk over to a different place to meet a friend...

...and then go outside to get some fresh air...

...and then go back to a different part of the club...

...and then back to the bar to refill their drinks...

...you get the idea.

It all seems so innocent. In fact, there's almost no touching involved. All they're asking the woman to do is MOVE from one place to another place within the same room. Again, it *seems* so innocent, but there's some deep psychology at play.

That's because, this "movement" from one place to another is subconsciously building intimacy and trust between the two people. Because after all, you only "travel" with people you know!

Is it sleazy?

When your goal is to bed a woman you just met...*yes!* (And again, I say that as a very, very happily married man).

But don't let the sleaziness behind the origin of this technique distract you from the powerful psychology that anchors it. The fact is, you want your subscribers to like you. You want them to trust you. And as long as you have their best interest in mind, there's nothing wrong with that.

So ask them to like you on Facebook...

Ask them to follow you on Twitter...

Ask them to whitelist your emails...

Ask them to read a recent blog post or watch a video on YouTube...

Have them do something...BOUNCE them around!

Because when they do...when they comply...you will have achieved something rather magical. You will have caused a change in someone's regular routine. Yes, it's a minor change, but it's a change none-the-less. And that change makes YOU an authority. That change makes YOU a friend. That change means that they can and should listen to you, and that's exactly what we're trying to accomplish in the Indoctrination Series.

To put it all in context, here's an example of a 2-part "Indoctrination Series." Notice how it "bounces" subscribers to different types of content, and "bounces" them off to your different social properties...

NOTE: Since this email is designed to be sent after your welcome email, it's best if the welcome mail that precedes this series includes a P.S. (or P.P.S.) that "opens a loop" teasing the fact that they're getting some of your best content. Here's an example P.S. you can swipe and add to your welcome email...

P.S. The next few days are gonna feel like Christmas...

Because as an added bonus for subscribing, I'm going to be sending you my "best of the best" [blog posts/articles/case studies/videos/tools/swipe file/etc.]

Tomorrow you're going to get the first of the "big three".

It's about [HINT AT BENEFIT AND END RESULT WITHOUT REVEALING THE EXACT TOPIC].

Stay tuned...it's gonna be good.

* * * * *

Message #1 – Sent 1 Day After Welcome Mail

* * * * *

Subj: *Here's your free gift (as promised)*

I promised yesterday that I would send you

one of our three most popular [blog posts/ articles/case studies/videos/tools/etc.]...

...but before I do that I wanted to introduce myself.

[INSERT PERSONAL PIC. IT CAN BE YOU WITH YOUR FAMILY OR YOU AT THE OFFICE WITH YOUR TEAM... WHATEVER IS APPROPRIATE. JUST MAKE SURE IT'S FUN AND SHOWS YOUR PERSONALITY]

That's a picture of me with [DESCRIBE PIC AND WHY IT'S SIGNIFICANT]

EXAMPLE #1: That's a picture of me with my family at our beach house. Purchasing this beach house was truly a dream come true, and now that you're a subscriber I want to help make your dream come true.

EXAMPLE #2: That's a picture of me with team at a recent office party. As you can see, we like to mix business with pleasure, because at the end of the day we love what we do! (And we're pretty dang good at it.) I look forward to putting this same passion and enthusiasm to work for you!

Ok, now that we're not strangers anymore... check this out:

[LINK TO BEST OF CONTENT #1]

This is the [blog post/article/case study/ video/swipe file/tool/etc.] I promised to send you.

You're gonna love it. It's about [HINT AT BENEFIT AND END RESULT WITHOUT REVEALING THE EXACT TOPIC].

Go [watch/read/download] it now, because there's more coming your way tomorrow...

Talk soon,

[YOUR NAME]

P.S. Ok, so I changed my mind...

Since I like to always under-promise and over-deliver, I'm going to go ahead and give you your second gift today instead of having to wait until tomorrow.

(See, it pays to read these messages from beginning to END.) :)

Here you go:

[LINK TO "BEST OF" CONTENT 2 OF 3]

Tomorrow your third gift will hit your inbox, so keep an eye out for this subject line: [INSERT SUBJECT LINE FOR NEXT EMAIL]

*****

Message #2 – Send 2 Days After Welcome Mail

*****

Subj: *Free Gift (3 of 3)*

Subj: *Here's your 3rd gift*

Subj: *Gift #3...as promised*

Yesterday you received:

Gift #1: [TITLE AND DESCRIPTION]

Gift #2: [TITLE AND DESCRIPTION]

...along with a silly picture of me [DESCRIPTION OF PICTURE FROM EMAIL #1].

So if you missed those, you might want to do a quick search in your inbox for this subject line: [INSERT SUBJECT LINE FOR BEST OF EMAIL #1]

Go ahead and do it now. I'll wait. :)

Now that you're caught back up, you need to check this out:

[LINK TO "BEST OF" CONTENT 3 OF 3]

I truly saved the best for last.

You're about to access [DESCRIBE THE BENEFIT OF CONTENT].

This is without a doubt the most popular [blog post/article/case study/video/swipe file/tool/etc.] I've ever released, and so I know you'll love it too.

So what are you waiting for?

Go [read/watch/download] it now!

Talk soon,

[YOUR NAME]

P.S. Like what you've seen in these last few messages?

Then good news!

[Every week/Twice a week/Every month] I send out more content just like this, so there's even more good stuff coming your way.

You can also see more of my archived content here:

[LINK TO ARCHIVES PAGE OR PILLAR POST PAGE ON BLOG IF YOU HAVE IT]

But here's the BIGGIE...

You need to make sure you whitelist my email address: [INSERT SEND FROM ADDRESS]

...and mark all my mails as "Important" if you're using Gmail.

```
Also, make sure you're following me on
Facebook and Twitter because I also announce
new content updates on those platforms, and
again I don't want you to miss out.

Join me on Facebook here: [LINK TO FACEBOOK
PAGE]

Follow me on Twitter here: [LINK TO TWITTER
PROFILE]
```

By deploying an Indoctrination Series like the one above, you will progress your new subscriber through the first phase of the relationship. They will shift from "stranger" to "friend," thus increasing the chance that they'll take the next step and become your customer or client.

And speaking of the "next step," that's what Phase 2 is all about...

Chapter 6:

Phase 2 – Engagement

Ok, so you have a new subscriber, and they're fully indoctrinated to you and your brand. You have "bounced" them all over the web to follow you on social media and consume different types of content, and your emails are landing in their priority inbox and getting opened with excitement and enthusiasm.

So now what?

It's simple...now it's time to make the sale.

But you can't rush it. If you move too quickly, you'll scare off your prospect. It's sort of like proposing marriage on a first date. It doesn't mean the person won't marry you at some point, but when you ask on the first date you just look like a creep, and the chances of getting a second date are practically ZERO.

So what do you do? How do you pivot to the sale? The answer is actually quite simple: You talk about whatever topic brought them to you in the first place.

Remember, the goal of an Engagement Series is to make an initial sale to a prospect that has shown interest in something. They've been segmented by opting in with their email address to receive that "something" and will now begin receiving an email series intended to sell them a product or service that corresponds with that interest.

We call that "something" a Lead Magnet.

What is a Lead Magnet?

Lead Magnets are critical because they are the entry point into an Engagement Series. The quality of your Lead Magnet is the #1 variable

in determining how fast your list will grow and whether someone will opt in to any particular Engagement Series to receive an offer.

So... what the heck is a Lead Magnet?

A Lead Magnet is simply a small "chunk" of value (usually content) that solves a SPECIFIC problem for a SPECIFIC market that is offered in exchange for an opt in.

Notice that I state the word SPECIFIC twice in the definition. The #1 mistake made with the Lead Magnet is that it is not specific enough, but we'll cover this and other factors of high-converting Lead Magnets in great detail later in this book. Don't worry; by the time I'm done with you, you'll have a Lead Magnet that steadily feeds leads into your Invisible Selling Machine.

Some common types of Lead Magnets include:

- Special Reports

- White Papers

- Case Studies

- Price Sheets

- Cheat Sheets

- Free downloads,

...you get the idea.

Again, it's the specific "chunk" of value you're giving away for free in exchange for your prospect's contact information and permission to follow-up with them in the future. But, make no mistake: Just because you're giving away this "chunk" of content for free, that doesn't mean that you can slack off and deliver a poor value or experience.

Never forget that a prospect's email address has value. So while this is not a monetary transaction, the prospect is giving you something very valuable when handing over their email address: their time and their attention. In other words, this is a transaction. It is a type of "sale." So treat it with respect, and above all else make sure that you are delivering value to your prospect over and above what they are delivering to you.

Leads are the fuel that drives your "machine." Treat them like gold, or your Machine will break down.

Ok, so now that you understand what a Lead Magnet is let's look at some examples. First off, you need to know that this is NOT a Lead Magnet...

SUBSCRIBE TO OUR FREE DAILY NEWSLETTER

Sure, you may think your newsletter is valuable, but to a brand-new visitor, all they think when they see this is, "Great...another email cluttering my inbox. No, thanks."

If you want to increase your opt in rates and get more leads and prospects on your list, you need to offer a SPECIFIC benefit to your target market...something you know they actually want. For example, this is a very successful Lead Magnet we have deployed in the past in the gardening/homesteading market...

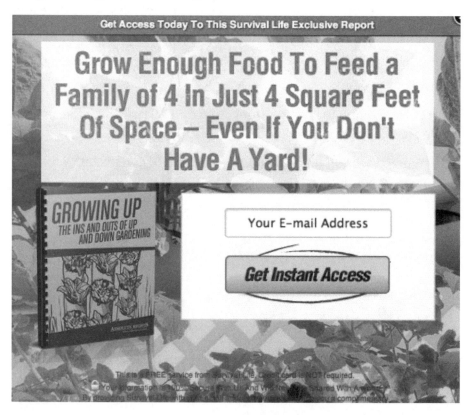

Notice the specificity of the offer being made. It isn't just: "How to Grow a Great Garden," or "10 Steps To an Amazing Garden." Instead, we're telling our subscriber SPECIFICALLY, "How To Grow Enough Food To Feed a Family of 4 In Just 4 Square Feet of Space...Even If you Don't Have a Yard!"

Wait, so how many people will this garden feed?

A family of 4!

And how much space is required?

Just 4 feet!

And what if I don't have a yard?

That's ok...you don't need one!

Do you see how this is infinitely more compelling than a whitepaper entitled, "The Better Growers Guide"...or even "How To Grow a Vertical Garden?"

THIS is how you win! This is your formula: Promise a SPECIFIC solution to a SPECIFIC problem, and your market will beat a path to your door.

The Entry-Point To Invisible Selling

Lead Magnets are also critical because they are the entry point into your Invisible Selling Machine. The very act of opting in to receive a Lead Magnet indicates interest in the topic of that Lead Magnet, which should trigger a new Engagement Series dedicated to that topic. This is just one more reason why SPECIFIC Lead Magnets are essential to the "Invisible Selling Machine" process. Without a specific Lead Magnet that's devoted to a specific topic, you don't know what you should offer your new-engaged subscriber.

For example, imagine you have three products in the golf niche, each of which appeals to a different desired end result:

- **Product 1** - Improves your drive

- **Product 2** - Improves your "short game"

- **Product 3** - Improves your putting

Each of these flagship products should have at least one Lead Magnet that speaks to the end result provided by each product. So for example, subscribers that opt in to a Lead Magnet about improving their putting have expressed interest in improving their putting game, and are perfect candidates for an Engagement Series that sells Product 3, whereas subscribers who opt in for a video on "The Magic Grip That Ads 10 Yards To Any Drive" should be added to an Engagement Series that sells Product 1.

Make sense?

We'll talk more about Lead Magnets as we progress through this book. Just know that not all Lead Magnets are created equal, so we'll look at the dos and don'ts of building high-converting Lead Magnets a bit later. For now, I just want you to have a taste of this important concept before we went any further.

What are you talking about?

Most email marketers blast messages about the same topic to the same list day after day.

Big mistake.

Smart email marketers know that a long-term email marketing strategy requires segmentation. You must change the message based on what you know about the subscriber or you risk burning out your list.

The Engagement Phase of the Invisible Selling Machine leverages what we know about a new lead to send them interest-based follow-up that promotes the right product or service.

How do we know what they're interested? Easy... the Lead Magnet tells us. If a new lead opts in for a Lead Magnet about gardening, it triggers a specific Engagement Series that sells products or services about gardening.

At Digital Marketer we have Lead Magnets about blogging, Facebook advertising, social media marketing and more. The act of downloading any one of these Lead Magnets triggers a separate

Engagement Series intended to continue the conversation about that particular topic.

This is the magic that makes the Invisible Selling Machine work. This is where the money is made.

As new leads enter your Invisible Selling Machine they only receive communications that are of interest to them. Novel concept, right?

Price determines length

It's a question I get all the time: "How long do I email a prospect about an offer?"

It's a good question and I have an answer but it's really more of a rule of thumb. This is your business and you know better than I the tolerance of your list and the intricacies of what you're offering. I can tell you that endlessly droning on about the same offer and topic email after email is a fantastic way to kill your list. Don't do that.

Here's the rule of thumb:

Price determines the duration of your Engagement Series.

You don't need to kill an ant with an atom bomb. You don't need a 30-day email series to sell a low-dollar product. If it's been 3-5 days and they haven't bought—it's ok. Let them drop out of that Engagement Series and back into a Segmentation Series and start talking to them about another topic.

We sell a lot of low-ticket, impulse buy offers and we typically email for 3-5 days (look out for the Flash Sale Series later in this book) for offers of this type. Anything much longer than this, while you might see a few more sales, does far more damage to the list than can be recouped with these minimal sales.

For products with a mid-range price point we typically set up a series that runs 5-10 days. High-ticket items can require up to a 21-day email series (or longer) but usually no less than 7 days. Again, these are just guidelines, and what defines "mid-range" and "high-ticket" can vary from market to market. The big takeaway is to consider the price point of your offer as you set up the length of your email series. The higher the price-point, the longer the follow-up series.

But enough talk about concepts, let's take a look at an actual Engagement Series.

Gain, Logic, Fear

This 3-part series can be deployed to anyone that opted in for a Lead Magnet but didn't buy your initial offer. It works because there are three primary reasons that people do just about anything:

- **Gain** – We move toward the things we want.

- **Logic** – We move toward what makes rational sense.

- **Fear** – We move away from the things that can harm us or toward something we think is going away.

Each email in this 3-part sequence focuses on one of the above starting with Gain.

Email 1 - Gain

The first email in the Gain/Logic/Fear follow-up series should begin with a curiosity-based subject line. As you can see from the examples below, I like to have a little fun. These types of subject lines aren't appropriate for all markets, but I would encourage you to push the envelope a bit and avoid "corporate speak" at all costs...

SUBJECT: Did you see this?

SUBJECT: Yep, this actually works

SUBJECT: BOOM! That just happened...

Then, you'll immediately remind them of the previous action they just took that got them on your list (i.e. opting in for the Lead Magnet).

Yesterday you requested my [insert Lead Magnet title/description here], and I just wanted to check back in and see if you had a chance to [read/watch] it yet.

This statement is powerful, because it's a subtle reminder of a commitment they previously made. Once a person makes a commitment, they are much more likely to remain consistent to the direction of that commitment when making future choices.

The email quickly transitions into discussing the gain or benefit surrounding your offer.

More importantly, I wanted to make sure you saw this:

LINK TO OFFER LANDING PAGE

If you're really serious about [insert topic/ known desired end result], then this is the ideal first step.

If you're making a low-dollar offer, it makes sense to mention it in the next section of the Gain email. But, you might want to tweak this closing if you're making a high-dollar offer.

Not only does it work, at only [insert price] it's the tiniest investment you can make and still have a realistic expectation of results.

So get it now while you can:

LINK TO OFFER LANDING PAGE

```
This price won't be available much longer, so
I would grab your copy now while it's still
fresh in your mind.


Talk soon,

[Name]
```

Notice that the last bit of this first email hints at a bit of scarcity by mentioning that the price could go up. You obviously don't want to say this if it isn't true, but if you're running a sale it can give your click-throughs and conversion rates a big boost.

Email 2 – Logic

Although it may seem illogical, the logic angle is the least effective of the three. (You might want to read that last sentence again just to make sure you got it.) While we like to think of ourselves as logical beings, the reality is most purchase decisions are made based on emotion (i.e. gain and fear), not logic. But the logic email is still important, because there are some prospects that will weigh all options and make a logical decision to purchase or not.

This group represents a smaller percentage of the market, but to ignore them completely would be a mistake. (And, frankly, if you can't make a logical argument as to why someone should take your offer... you really have no business making the offer in the first place.)

Try one of these subject lines on this second email of the series...

SUBJECT: Call me crazy, but...

SUBJECT: Really...really!!

SUBJECT: Frankly I'm a little surprised

These subject lines start to press the prospect a bit and you can certainly tweak those to be more congruent with your circumstances.

Then, we hit them with some logic...

```
Hi [NAME],

I must say I'm a little surprised you still
haven't taken me up on this:

LINK TO OFFER LANDING PAGE

If you really want to [insert known desired
end result] (and I'm guessing you do or you
wouldn't have even visited my site), then
this is the ideal first step.
```

Do you see the logical argument? It's the part that reads, "...and I'm guessing you do or you wouldn't have even visited my site...". This phrase hits the logical minded buyer right where they live. Then, we return to the benefit and the desired end result as we close the email.

```
Remember, not only will it get you [insert
specific benefit provided by the offer here],
but it will also give you the momentum you
desperately need to achieve [insert broad-
based desired end result].

So DO IT NOW before it gets lost in the
shuffle of life.

Talk soon,

[Your Name]
```

Easy peasy. We know they're interested in the topic (after all, they opted in for the Lead Magnet) so we keep these emails short and punchy. We just want them to click to the sales page.

Email 3 – Fear

On day three we turn up the heat by deploying the fear of loss. We have two versions of this last email in the series. The first is for offers that have a true deadline or some element of scarcity. It might be a limited quantity, a closing date or a looming price increase or a sale that's ending. In any case, use a subject line like...

SUBJECT: Last chance?

SUBJECT: Bad news

SUBJECT: You're about to miss out

If your offer contains true scarcity, use this version:

Yep, this is pretty much your last chance to get [insert offer name] at this price:

LINK TO OFFER LANDING PAGE

On [insert date] the [price is going up to $XX -OR- offer is closing], so you better get it now, because chances are you won't see it again [at this price] for quite some time.

Good Luck,
[NAME]

If you don't have true scarcity in your offer use this instead,

This is it... I'm done talking to you about this:

LINK TO OFFER LANDING PAGE

For the last few days I've been encouraging you to get in while you can, but now time is up. After today, you won't hear me talking about it any longer.

So this is your last chance.

Get in now, or risk missing out completely:

LINK TO OFFER LANDING PAGE

```
All the best,

[YOUR NAME]
```

Lastly, I like to tack a bit of a logic argument to the end of this last email using the P.S.,

```
P.S. Remember, not only will it get you
[insert specific benefit provided by the offer
here], but it will also give you the momentum
you desperately need to achieve [insert
broad-based desired end result].

Get off the fence and get started NOW:

LINK TO OFFER LANDING PAGE
```

This Gain, Logic, Fear Series is one of my favorite Engagement campaigns because it just flat out works. We've tried it in every business from web-based software and publishing companies, to brick and mortar shoe stores and acupuncturists, and without exception it has given sales a boost.

But despite its effectiveness, some prospects still won't buy from this series. And that's ok! Your Engagement Series doesn't have to end here. In fact, we frequently extend our Engagement campaigns by stacking a Gain/Logic/Fear series with an "Are You Still? / Have You Yet?" series...

Stop biting your fingernails!

Listen carefully because I'm about to give you a powerful follow-up campaign that you can set up in 5 minutes. This campaign, even when done as poorly as I'm about to show you, has a tremendous effect on sales.

A good friend and business partner of mine is a chronic nail biter. I mean the kind that bites the nail right down to the cuticle. So, one day he hops on Google looking for a solution to his problem and he finds this website...

So, he opts in to the Lead Magnet to get the free report and he's made an immediate offer for a product that will end his nail biting habit. He, like most new leads, declined the offer. But the owner of this website didn't give up...

A few days later he gets an email from this website with the subject line, "*Still biting your nails?*"

The body of the email was simple. The marketer reiterated what my buddy already knew: biting your nails is a disgusting habit. But despite this seemingly logical argument, my friend declined the offer once again. But the emails didn't stop...

A week later he received another email, again with the *exact same* subject line and the *exact same* body copy, "*Still biting your nails?*"

My friend still didn't buy, so the emails kept coming...

Every week...week after week...my friend received this *exact same* email with the *exact same* subject line *("Still biting your nails?")* until one day he'd had enough. The email hit his inbox at the exact moment he was biting his nails, and that was all it took. He plunked down the cash for the product...invisible selling had worked.

A Slightly More Elegant Solution...

Let me be perfectly clear...

The story above illustrates an extreme and inelegant use of the "Are you still?" email campaign. The campaign would almost certainly yield better results (and be considerable less obnoxious) if they switched up the email body copy... or at least the subject line. But it's certainly better than nothing, which is exactly what most would have done.

So...why does it work?

Why is the "Are you still?" campaign so effective?

It's simple: nobody likes to feel stuck. Your prospect arrived at your website or called your office because they have a problem that needs a solution. And they took the first step of requesting your Lead Magnet because they're serious, and they believe that you have a solution to their problem.

So make no mistake: they're stuck.

If they had the solution, they wouldn't have found you in the first place. They're stuck, and they want to get unstuck. So if you want to give your sales a boost, all you have to do is tell them they're stuck. Twist the knife ever-so-gently while reminding them that you have the solution, and you'll move them to action. And that's exactly what the "Are you still?" campaign does...

...it twists the knife, but it does it without being obnoxious or "in your face."

Another variation of the "Are you still?" campaign is the "Have you yet?" campaign. The psychology behind this campaign is identical, so you can use this version to mix up your messages so you aren't repeating the exact same email over and over again like our friend with the nail-biting site.

Here are some example subject lines using the "Have you yet?" structure:

- Have you lost those 10 pounds yet? – Weight Loss

- Have you broke 90 yet? – Golfers

- Did you run that marathon yet? – Runners

- Have you finished your website yet? – Marketers

- Have you whitened your teeth yet? - Dentists

...you get the idea.

Again, the formula is simple: Remind your prospect that they're stuck while simultaneously reminding them that you have the solution. Do that, and your sales will increase with every email you send.

Stacking campaigns

The two Engagement Series I've covered in this chapter (Gain, Logic, Fear and "Are you still? / Have you yet?") work well when they are stacked on top of each other.

Here's what a series might look like if you added an "Are you still? Have you yet?" campaign on top of the Gain, Logic, Fear campaign.

- **Day 0** – On the day they opt in for the Lead Magnet, you'll send them a welcome email with access information for the Lead Magnet itself.

- **Day 1** – G/L/F Email #1 (Gain)

- **Day 2** – G/L/F Email #2 (Logic)

- **Day 3** – G/L/F Email #3 (Fear)

- **Day 7** – Are you still? / Have you yet? (First Attempt)

- **Day 14** – Are you still? / Have you yet? (Second Attempt)

- **Day 21** – Are you still? / Have you yet? (Third Attempt)

The timing of these emails can be adjusted in whatever way you see fit, but the big takeaway here is that you can stack email campaigns upon email campaigns to lengthen the series.

Are you seeing the power of an interest-based Engagement Series?

Are you starting to see that this is something you can do, even if you aren't an experienced email copywriter?

If so, then you're well on your way to building your Invisible Selling Machine. Now things start getting really interesting...

Chapter 7:

Phase 3 – Ascension

Ok, the "Machine" is doing its job. It's turning strangers into friends and friends into customers. But, while acquiring a buyer is good, acquiring a multi-buyer is where the real money is made. And assuming what you're offering is valuable, you'll find that once you get that first sale, it's much easier to get the second, third, fourth...

Here's why this works...

The Value Loop: Engagement + Ascension

Broke marketers make a single offer and call it a day when they get a sale. Wealthy marketers maximize profit by making another offer. And another. And another.

It's called the Value Loop.

Here's the thing (and this is a "writer downer") ...

For every offer you make there is some percentage of buyers who would buy more.

Read that again because it's important. It's the key insight in creating the Value Loop.

- For every McDonald's value meal ordered, some percentage will Super Size the fry and drink.

- For every air conditioning repair, some percentage will buy a yearly maintenance plan.

- For every training course sold, some percentage will buy high-dollar one-on-one consulting.

It's not magic. It's not trickery. You must provide value above and beyond what it costs your customer to create a Value Loop. But the majority of business owners I know provide tremendous value, and yet they have no Value Loop in place. They make a single offer to their prospects and that's the end of it.

Ascending your customers into a Value Loop is as simple as making another offer. It amazes me how many businesses fail to do this.

Successful businesses understand that customers are wanting (actually they are demanding) an upgraded experience. They want more value from you...so give it to them!

Types of Ascension

When you combine great products and services with well-executed Engagement and Ascension, everyone wins and your business will grow exponentially.

Here are some methods of Ascension[1]...

- **Immediate Upsells** – Offering a product or service with the same desired end result as the prior purchase.

- **Cross-Sells** – Offering a product or service with a related desired end result to the prior purchase.

---

1 Students of Digital Marketer's Customer Value Optimization (CVO) process will recognize these methods of Ascension as the Profit Maximizer stage of the CVO process. Learn more about the Customer Value Optimization process here: http://digitalmarketer.com/start-here/

- **Bundles and Kits** – Offering multiple products in a package to create a new value proposition.

- **Affiliate/CPA Offers** – Offering a similar or related product as an affiliate to earn a commission from the sale.

- **Premium Subscription** – Offering a product or service with recurring billing.

The Ultimate Upsell Formula: Speed & Automation

The most effective Ascension offers contain either one or both of the following: *speed and automation*. If you can make an offer to a buyer that speeds up and/or automates their ability to get the benefit from the initial thing they bought—you've got a winning Ascension offer.

After all, they've already indicated interest in gaining a particular benefit. Offering something that achieves that benefit faster and easier is an obvious upsell.

Here are some types of Speed and Automation Upsells

- Software/Application

- Done For You Service

- Audit/Strategy Session

- Private Labeling

- Templates/Themes

- Supplements

- Equipment/Tools

Speed and automation upsells are the easiest to create as well because it's a natural extension of the products and services you're already selling. And, more importantly, speed and automation upsells are easy to sell with a simple Ascension Series. Let's take a look at a simple but very effective Ascension campaign that you might recognize from the last chapter of this book.

The Offer Upgrade Campaign

This campaign is very similar to the Gain, Logic, Fear campaign detailed in the chapter on Engagement. In this campaign, we'll use a 3-part email series that employs the same principles of...

- **Gain** – We move toward the things we want.

- **Logic** – We move toward what makes rational sense.

- **Fear** – We move away from the things that can harm us or toward something we think is going away.

The big difference is that we'll be referencing their prior purchase (rather than their prior opt in for the Lead Magnet) throughout this series.

Email 1 – Gain

Once again, the first email uses a curiosity based subject line...

SUBJECT: Did you miss this?

SUBJECT: It works even better with THIS

SUBJECT: Wait! You forgot something...

We lead off similarly to the Gain, Logic, Fear campaign in that we acknowledge their prior commitment. Again, the big difference being that, in this Ascension Series, we are acknowledging a prior purchase rather than the opt in for a Lead Magnet.

```
Yesterday you purchased [insert product
name], and I just wanted to say thanks again
for your order.

I'm so happy to have you in the family.

More importantly, I wanted to make sure you
saw this:

LINK TO UPSELL SALES PAGE
```

The email transitions into the desired end result or gain associated with your upsell offer. Remember, if you want maximum results from your upsell you'll need to be speaking to the same desired end result that is associated with their prior purchase.

The big difference is that you're focusing on the speed and automation of that result.

```
If you're really serious about [insert topic/
known desired end result], then this is the
ideal next step.

Not only will it get you [known desired end
result], it will get you there much, MUCH
[faster/easier/with less work].

So get it now while you can:

LINK TO UPSELL SALES PAGE

This [price/offer/product] won't be available
much longer, so I would grab your copy now
while it's still fresh in your mind.

Talk soon,

[Name]
```

Notice the language used, "Not only will it get you [known desired end result], it will get you there much, MUCH [faster/easier/with less work.]" That is a speed and automation offer and it's very powerful.

Email 2 – Logic

The second email gives the customer a logical reason to upgrade. Use a subject line like...

SUBJECT: Call me crazy, but...

SUBJECT: THIS is the logical next step

SUBJECT: Frankly I'm a little surprised

The body of this email is nearly identical to the Gain, Logic, Fear campaign from the Engagement Phase. Notice that we quite literally state that this is the "logical next step" after purchasing the prior offer.

> Call me crazy, but I'm a little surprised you still haven't taken me up on this:
>
> LINK TO UPSELL SALES PAGE
>
> If you really want to [insert known desired end result] (and I'm guessing you do or you wouldn't have purchased [insert product name]), then this is the logical next step.

This second email closes by restating the known desired end result associated with the offer.

> Remember, not only will it get you [insert specific benefit provided by the product they just purchased here], but it will also give you the momentum you desperately need to achieve [insert broad-based desired end result].
>
> So DO IT NOW before it gets lost in the shuffle of life.
>
>
> Talk soon,
>
> [Name]

Email 3 – Fear

Just as in the Gain, Logic, Fear series, on the last day we're going to push a bit harder by employing scarcity in the subject line and body copy to move anyone that's sitting on the fence to action.

SUBJECT: Last chance?

SUBJECT: Bad news

SUBJECT: You're about to miss out

If you have true scarcity (a limited number of seats, a deadline, etc.) use this version.

Yep, this is pretty much your last chance to get [insert product name] at this price:

LINK TO UPSELL SALES PAGE

On [insert date] the [price is going up to $XXX -OR- offer is closing], so you better get it now, because chances are you won't see it again [at this price] for quite some time.

Good Luck,

[NAME]

P.S. Remember, not only will it get you [insert specific benefit provided by the product they just purchased here], but it will also give you the momentum you desperately need to achieve [insert broad-based desired end result].

Get off the fence and get started NOW:

LINK TO UPSELL SALES PAGE

But, if you don't have true scarcity you can use this modified version.

This is it…I'm done talking to you about this:

LINK TO UPSELL SALES PAGE

For the last few days I've been encouraging you to get in while you can, but now time is up. After today, you won't hear me talking about it any longer.

So this is your last chance.

Get in now, or risk missing out completely:

LINK TO UPSELL SALES PAGE

All the best,

[YOUR NAME]

P.S. Remember, not only will it get you [insert specific benefit provided by the product they just purchased here], but it will also give you the momentum you desperately need to achieve [insert broad-based desired end result].

Get off the fence and get started NOW:

LINK TO UPSELL SALES PAGE

Once you have an Ascension series (or two) in place, the next step is to create a series for your leads and prospects that DON'T ascend. Fortunately, that's what the next phase is all about...

Chapter 8:

Phase 4 – Segmentation

Ok, so you have subscribers on your email list, but how do you determine which offer to make them?

The answer: Segmentation.

List segmentation is critical to maintaining a healthy email list with high engagement and a low unsubscribe rate. The fact, is continuing to send a subscriber emails about a topic when they are not engaged (i.e. opening, clicking, buying, opting in, etc.) is the fastest way to lose that subscriber.

The Segmentation phase of the Invisible Selling Machine is the linchpin that holds the entire process together. If you can get segmentation right, you'll make more money, send less emails, and build tremendous good will amongst your subscribers.

Autoresponders vs. Broadcast

Let's start by defining the two different methods you can use to send email:

- **Autoresponders** – Sending emails automatically based on a set schedule that begins when the prospect opts in to the list.

Example: A 7-day autoresponder will automatically send one email per day for 7 days following the initial opt in.

- **Broadcasts** – Sending an email one time to everyone on a list (or segment of a list) at that moment in time. Example: An email written to promote webinar registration and sent to everyone on a list at one time.

Autoresponders are truly "set it and forget it" and that's the beauty of using them. They are very flexible. They can be set to send email for two days, skip a day, and then send email for 3 more days. They can be set to send at specific times and on specific days of the week. In fact, if you were so inclined, you could setup an autoresponder series to send a different email for months...even YEARS into the future. We don't recommend this strategy, but with the right autoresponder solution, it is possible.

Broadcast email allows you to be timelier with your email messages, and allows you to test the performance of an email before it becomes part of an autoresponder sequence. After all, what's the point of automating something if it isn't working?

So, which does the Invisible Selling Machine use?

I've heard the case for taking both extremes. Some so-called "experts" teach that you should never send autoresponder series because you can't be topical or timely with everything set on autopilot.

Others argue the exact opposite.

They'll tell you to write all your emails in one sitting, set them on autopilot and retire to your yacht in the Caribbean.

I've tested both—neither works.

As is so often the case in life, it's a balance between autoresponders and broadcast email that gets results. That said, most of the phases of The Invisible Selling Machine are better suited to autoresponders than broadcast email.

For the most part, autoresponder series are used for:

- Indoctrination
- Engagement
- Ascension
- Reengagement

And that's what makes the Segmentation phase of your machine different. Segmentation is the only phase of the Invisible Sales Machine dominated by broadcast email. To be more specific, segmentation emails are broadcast to any subscriber not currently receiving an Engagement or Ascension Series.

Stop Selling...Start Segmenting

The Segmentation Phase of your Invisible Selling Machine has one job: **To segment subscribers into a relevant Engagement Series.**

Why? Because that's where the money is made!

The biggest mistake I see marketers make is sending blanket promotions to everyone on their list. Not only is it ineffective, it's also a recipe for high spam complaints and high unsubscribes. So stop doing it! Instead, give your leads and prospects an opportunity to "raise their hand" and express interest in a particular topic.

And when they do (by either opting in for a new Lead Magnet, calling into your office, etc.) then you can segment them into an Engagement Series where the actual selling can take place.

This is ultra-important so I'm going to say it again: You don't monetize your list by sending email broadcasts. You monetize your list by 1) segmenting active, interested leads into relevant sub-lists (i.e. Engagement series) and then 2) allowing the Engagement Series to do the selling.

This is a "value first" strategy because with this method, you offer something of value (i.e. a Lead Magnet) to your prospect. If they request it, you then have permission to follow-up with them about the topic of that Lead Magnet. If they don't request the Lead Magnet, you don't talk to them anymore about that topic, because they have already told you they aren't that interested in it.

Make sense?

This is how you create a sustainable email marketing machine.

And it's not just for web-based companies, either. If you have a purely off-line business, use your Segmentation emails to get them to call in to request information, or come by your store. The big takeaway is that asking your subscribers to raise their hand FIRST just flat out works.

Date Night

But I know what you're thinking, "Ryan, if they're already on my list, why would I have them opt in AGAIN?" Two reasons:

> **1. Permission is NEVER assumed.** Just because someone expressed interest in you or your brand once, that doesn't give you the right to talk to them about whatever the heck you want to talk about whenever you want to talk about it. Sure, you may legally be allowed to do it (or not, by the way...laws vary from country to country and change frequently, so none of this should be construed as legal advice), but that doesn't mean you *should* do it. If you want to keep spam complaints down and engagement rates up, it's always best that you focus your follow-up on what your prospects want, rather than what you want.

> **2. It re-consummates the relationship.** What was the original action they took to get on your email list in the first place? They opted in for something, right? If you ask them to repeat this process every now and then, it actually improves the long-term health of your subscriber list. It's sort of like when married couples have a "date night"...

I've been happily married for over 12 years, and I'm convinced that the smartest thing my wife and I ever did was to institute a "Date Night." Date Night is sacred. Every Thursday night, unless one of us is sick or traveling, we go out on a date just like we used to do before we tied the knot.

Do I need to take my wife on a date? I guess not. I mean, we're married, right, so what's the point? The point is, every time we have a date night, our marriage is strengthened. It reminds us of what life was like before we had 4 kids, and it allows us to focus on each other and our marriage.

It's good for us!

And the same is true for you and your subscribers. You need to take them on a date every now and then. They need to be reminded of what brought you two together in the first place (i.e. opting in for a Lead Magnet, calling into your office, walking into your store, etc.).

In short, they need to re-live the "engagement process."

I know the concept of a "date night" sounds a little trite and hokey when applied to email marketing, but trust me...it works! And you should try it! All you have to do is use your email broadcasts to deliver value FIRST, and when they accept your invitation, just add them to a custom Engagement Series. Do this, and you and your subscribers will live happily ever after.

Ok, enough pie-in-the-sky mumbo-jumbo...let's talk about how you actually DO IT. Here's a sample Segmentation Series you can model for your own list...

Segmenting With Content (i.e. The Goodwill Campaign)

This email series is known as a "Goodwill Campaign" because it leverages content (i.e. gives value first) and creates a feeling of goodwill for everyone on your list...even those who do not engage with the topic.

The sequence looks like this...

- **Email 1: Blind** - The first email is "blind" to the topic and instead uses curiosity to encourage engagement in the email.

- **Email 2: Direct** - The second email in the series is "direct," meaning it gets straight to the point by outlining the topic and its benefits.

- **Email 3: Content** - This final email in the series contains a call to action to access free and valuable information.

Now that you understand the role of each email in the series, let's look at them so you can see how they function as a complete campaign...

The first email in the series is intended to segment the subscribers who are particularly excited about you and your brand. In other words, the subscribers who respond to this email will be your biggest fans. They will be excited about the topic simply because YOU are excited about the topic. And you'll know this to be true, because the email will never reference the topic of your Lead Magnet.

Here's the email so you can see what I mean.

Goodwill Campaign: Email #1 (Blind)

First, we want to leverage a blind (i.e. curiosity-based) subject line. Something like...

```
Subj: Kinda weird but very [insert relevant
benefit - ex. "profitable" or "influential"]

Subj: This flat out WORKS!

Subj: One word... [insert relevant word - ex.
"spectacular" or "delightful"]
```

The email itself is super-short, because again, you don't have to "sell" the topic. Right now, we just want to find out who will segment themselves on the basis of YOUR interest and excitement alone. Here's the message...

```
If you're on my email list, it's fair to
assume you [DESCRIBE INTEREST OR BENEFIT -
ex. ... want to play the guitar"/ "... want to
get more clients"]

If so, this is the ideal next step:

[LINK TO LANDING PAGE]

Check it out...you'll be glad you did.

Talk soon,

[YOUR NAME]
```

Yep, that's it.

There's nothing about the topic at all. Just a promise from you that if they take action, they'll "be glad they did." And again, the only subscribers who are going to respond to this are your biggest fans. For everyone else, there's the second email in the "Goodwill Campaign"...

Goodwill Campaign: Email #2 (Direct)

The second email in the Goodwill Campaign is everything the first one was not. While the first message was "blind," the second one is centered around the Lead Magnet topic and the benefits of taking action. It all starts with a direct-on subject line...

```
Subj: Presenting...[topic / product name /
Lead Magnet name]

Subj: Special Report: [Lead Magnet Name]

Subj: Free Download: [Lead Magnet Name]
```

Subj: Case Study: [Case Study Name]

The email itself is, again, fairly brief because there's little buildup and there's nothing to sell. You're simply highlighting the topic of the Lead Magnet, and encouraging them to go to a landing page to request it.

Hi [NAME],

Have you ever wanted to [insert known objective or desired end result]?

Well now is your chance:

[LINK TO LANDING PAGE]

Recently I [wrote/recorded/rolled out a report/video/training/widget] [about/that does] [DESCRIBE TOPIC/PRODUCT] and I want you to have [a copy/it/one].

You can [access/get/buy] it right now at:

[LINK TO LANDING PAGE]

But do it now while it's fresh on your mind...

Talk soon,

[YOUR NAME]

NOTE: Don't let the call-to-action confuse you. This message could easily to be modified to drive inbound calls or encourage people to "swing by" your store on a specific day.

Goodwill Campaign: Email #3 (Content)

The last email in the B.D.C. Campaign is simple. All you're doing is providing access to valuable content that's related to the topic of the series. The role of this email is to segment off your "fence-sitters"... the people who are interested in the topic...they want to see you take the first step. And that's where the content comes into play...

With this email, you are truly giving value first, either through a blog post, an article, a free video or some other form of information or entertainment that they can consume *without* having to make a purchase or even fill out a form.

There are two ways to deliver this content to your subscribers:

> **1. Partial Push.** In a "partial push" email, the message simply describes the content and requires a click to your blog (or elsewhere) to consume it.

> **2. Full Push.** In a "full push" email, the entirety of the content can be viewed within the email itself. This works fine for text-based content such as email newsletters, but obviously if you're wanting to offer video, audio or other multi-media content you will need to opt for a "partial push" email.

If you're using "partial push," your email will contain copy like...

```
I've written a brand spanking new article
about [TOPIC/DESIRED RESULT] that I know
you're going to love.

You'll learn: [INSERT BULLETED LIST OF
TOPICS/BENEFITS]

Access it here: [LINK TO CONTENT]
```

But remember, the purpose of the content is not simply to provide content. (This is still a business, after all.) That's why, whether you go with the "partial push" or the "full push" method, you need to deploy multiple calls-to-action that drive your readers to the same landing page we used back in emails #1 and #2.

Here are a few ways you can do this without getting overly "salesy" in your content:

> 1. Linking from within the content to the landing page itself.

(NOTE: Here's one of our blog posts so you can see this method in action: http://www.digitalmarketer.com/6-million/)

2. Placing an image ad (a.k.a. banner ad) either inside or below the content

3. Adding an "oh by the way" to the P.S. to the bottom of your message. (For example: "P.S. If you like this article, you're going to love the free report I'm offering over at...")

So which call-to-action should you deploy in your content? Ideally, as many as possible! While there are certainly more aggressive ways to segment your list, the "Goodwill Campaign" is a fantastic series you can use week after week if you have fresh content to promote. Best of all, you'll accomplish the task of segmentation and make your subscribers love you in the process.

"Borrowing" Authority

The "Goodwill Campaign" is highly effective...but what if you don't have content? Or, what if you don't have a piece of content that is relevant to the Lead Magnet you've been promoting?

No worries.

Simply find a highly credible source that has created a piece of content (article, video, podcast, etc.) that's relevant to your Lead Magnet. Choose something that supports or strengthens the stance you take in the Lead Magnet so you can piggyback off of the authority of this 3rd party source.

For example, if you are promoting a Lead Magnet that covers how to start a business without raising capital from investors (a.k.a. "bootstrapping") a quick query in Google like this one...

site:wsj.com bootstrapping

... will return relevant articles written by the Wall Street Journal on the subject of "bootstrapping" a start-up business. In fact, I ran that very search and here's what Google returned...

And it's not just the Wall Street Journal. This technique will work for any reputable news source. Here are a couple more examples so you can see what I mean:

site:nytimes.com keyword

site:techcrunch.com keyword

site:[yourfavoritenewssite.com] keyword

This is one of the easiest emails to write because you simply explain the content, build a bit of excitement around it and drop a link to the news story. Try a subject line like...

Subj: *[NEWS SOURCE] LOVES/HATES [TOPIC]*

And use body copy like...

```
Did you know that according to the Wall
Street Journal bootstrapping a start up
business leads to a 75% greater probability
of success in the first year of the business?
```

The downside to this technique is you are linking to someone else's site instead of your own, making it impossible to insert your advertisements and calls-to-action within the content itself. But it's better than nothing, and you can still drop a call-to-action in the P.S.

of your email (which is actually one of the most-read parts of any message).

More importantly, your subscribers will thank you for sending them the content...even though they know you didn't write it. And even if you don't make the sale today, you're building up a store of goodwill that will almost certainly pay dividends in the future. But content isn't the only way to segment your list. You can also use good ol' fashioned surveys...

Segmenting With a Survey

Surveys are a fantastic method of segmentation. Regardless of your industry, your prospect's pain points and interests change from time to time. A survey allows your prospect to communicate that interest and segment themselves into an Engagement Series.

We call this this email survey campaign the "Help Me, Help You" series. The campaign opens with a question-based subject line such as...

Subj: *What's your BIGGEST problem?*

Subj: *Are you stuck?*

Let them know that the survey will be quick and easy. You can use a free survey-building program like SurveyMonkey.com (that's what we use) or Wufoo.com.

Use survey questions that uncover the interest, pain point or intent of the subscriber like...

- If I could help you with one thing that would enable your business to move faster and get UNSTUCK, what would it be? (This is an open ended question)

- What areas of [TOPIC] do you want to see us cover more? [Make this multiple choice and provide responses that segment your subscribers appropriately)

- If you could have a private conversation with me, what two questions would you ask? (Another open ended question)

Follow-up with a second and third email to maximize response on your survey. Tell them they're helping to drive future content. Make them a part of the process. And, of course, the last email should use a bit of urgency to let them know that this is their last chance to give you their opinion.

Once you have this survey data you can use it to make relevant offers to your list by segmenting subscribers into the appropriate Engagement Series. Or, use the data to determine the next product or service you'll create. Either way, you'll be talking to your list about the things that interest them, and that's the foundation of "Invisible Selling."

Segmenting with a Webinar

Webinars are another great way to segment your list, because if a subscriber is interested enough in a topic to attend an online event, there's a good chance they want to hear more about that topic. In our testing, we've found that a 3-day webinar promotion works best—with the webinar occurring on the 3rd day of the promotion. We've found that each day added to the promotion (beyond three days) adds registrants but decreases the show-up rate significantly. Here's how the campaign breaks down:

- **Email 1** – This email is direct. Use a subject line like "Special Training On [Topic of Webinar]" with a list of the benefits of attending the webinar.

- **Email 2** – Inject a bit of urgency and scarcity in this second email by using the date in the subject line. Something like, "Special Training on [DATE]" should do the trick. Don't forget to lay out the benefits of attendance again in this email.

- **Email 3** – This last email is scarcity based and we literally send this to anyone that hasn't registered 15 minutes before the event starts. Use a subject line like, "[STARTING NOW] We're all waiting on YOU!" You'll be amazed at how many last minute registrants you'll get, and the show-up rate will be very high on these late coming registrations.

Lastly—and this is a biggie—send a wrap-up email within one hour of the webinar's conclusion that summarizes the webinar and links to any offers that were made on the webinar. We call this the "Clean Up" campaign, and it typically doubles the sales we get during the webinar itself.

Also, it's worth noting that the term "webinar" isn't well received in all markets. Some have no idea what a "webinar" is, and others know what it is and don't like it. In those cases, you may want to use another term such as:

- Online Training

- Online Seminar

- Teleclass

Segmenting with a Blog

If you have a blog, this can be a go-to campaign that you deploy every month, because in addition to generating revenue, this campaign also generates a lot of goodwill with your subscribers. It's called a "Blog Launch," and it centers around a series of three blog posts each of which drives readers from the post into an Engagement Series by asking them to opt in to a Lead Magnet or buy a low-ticket offer.

Here's how the campaign is structured...

- **Email 1** – Use this email to set the stage for the "big idea" that will be covered in the three blog posts. Any in-depth teaching post will work, but we've found that a Case Study article works best here. Use copy like "I just finished an in-depth case study where I [SHOW YOU/OUTLINE/TELL YOU, etc.] [WHAT YOU ACCOMPLISHED]

- **Email 2** – The second email (and article on the blog) delivers the "How and Wow." The content should be very tactical – showing them EXACTLY how to achieve some desired end result. Say something like "In today's blog post, I break down the X steps you need to take to get/achieve [DESIRED END RESULT]

- **Email 3** – Use the third email (and piece of blog content) to overcome an objection to the eventual offer or generate controversy and conversation. It's a bonus if you can manage both goals with the same article, but creating controversy should be the primary goal if you can manage it. Controversial content has a higher chance of spreading virally and generating an avalanche of traffic to your site, but don't force it. Controversy is like dynamite. Used improperly, it can easily do more harm than good.

NOTE: You can see an example of the content we use for a Blog Launch Campaign on the Digital Marketer blog here: http://www. digitalmarketer.com/6-million

There should be no opt in or purchase necessary to get this content, and each blog posts should be interlinked and contain a call to action to a Lead Magnet or a deeply discounted low-dollar offer. The idea is to "bounce" them (see the section on "bouncing" in the Indoctrination Phase of the Invisible Selling Machine) from one article to another.

The Blog Launch campaign emails should also open loops (See the section on "opening loops" in the Indoctrination Phase of the Invisible Selling Machine) to create anticipation for the next article in the series. For example, you can open a loop in the P.S. of the first email of this series like this…

```
P.S. There was so much I wanted to cover on
this topic that it wouldn't all fit in one
post, so I'm breaking it up into three posts.

But don't worry… you won't have to wait a
week or more for Part 2 and Part 3.
```

> I'm putting the finishing touches on Part 2
> now, and I'll email you tomorrow and let you
> know when it's published. In the meantime, be
> sure to read Part 1: [LINK TO BLOG POST #1]

Put the Blog Launch campaign to work for you, I think you'll find that it generates tremendous goodwill while segmenting your broadcast list.

When Not to Segment

The goal of the Invisible Selling Machine is to move sales leads into the Engagement Phase and ultimately the Ascension Phase to sell them additional products and services. The Segmentation Phase is all about determining the right offer that will get your un-engaged leads into an Engagement Series.

As a general rule—any subscriber actively receiving an Engagement or Ascension Series should not receive Segmentation emails. After all, you don't want to distract them from the current offer. But there are two exceptions:

- **EXCEPTION #1: Content** – Subscribers join your list to get entertainment or information, so give it to them no matter where they are in your Invisible Selling Machine. I recommend sending content to your list (either in the form of a blog post or email newsletter) once or twice per week.

- **EXCEPTION #2: New Flagship Product** – These are rare, but when you're doing a big launch of a new product, the whole list gets it. Yes, this means you will be distracting some of your engaged subscribers, but when it's a brand-new, flagship offer... it's probably worth it.

Sales as Segmentation

So far we've only talked about free Lead Magnets as a method of Segmentation, but a low-dollar, impulse buy offer[2] can also be a great way to segment your broadcast list. Just remember that you should always approach your Segmentation broadcasts with a "value first" mentality, so if you're going to ask for money, you need to make them a truly incredible deal and not just an ordinary promotion.

For this type of Segmentation you can use a "Flash Sale Series." The Flash Sale is designed to activate new buyers on your broadcast list and reactivate those that haven't purchased in a while. By deeply discounting a product or service, you'll see a lot of action in a short amount of time.

And in the immortal words of Louie Anderson (in one of the funniest movies of all time), *"That's when the big bucks start rollin' in."* (P.S. Send me a tweet @RyanDeiss if you got that obscure movie reference.)

So, without further ado, here is the Flash Sale Series in its entirety...

Segmentation SERIES – Flash Sale

The purpose of the "Flash Sale" campaign is to segment subscribers based on a low dollar purchase instead of a free opt in.

* * * * *

Message #1:

* * * * *

Subj: *[FLASH SALE] The Ultimate [TRAINING/ PRODUCT]...*

---

2 Those familiar with Digital Marketer's Customer Value Optimization (CVO) process will recognize these low-dollar, impulse buy offers as Tripwire offers. You can learn more about the Customer Value Optimization process here: http://www.digitalmarketer.com/start-here/

Are you frustrated by [INSERT REASON TO BE FRUSTRATED RELATED TO PRODUCT/TRAINING. Ex "the lack of traffic or leads you're getting from Facebook]?

I was too, which is why I [CREATED/SOURCED/PUBLISHED/PRODUCTED/ETC.] [NAME OF PRODUCT/TRAINING], the [SOLUTION TO FRUSTRATION POINT ABOVE. Ex - "definitive, step-by-step formula for turning "fans" into customers"].

Get yours now:

[LINK TO SALESPAGE]

Normally these [TRAINING/PRODUCT TYPES] sell for $[XX] - $[XX], but for a limited time you can get this for just $[XX].

Yep, just $[XX]! That's over [X]%!

No trials… no subscriptions… no shenanigans…

…I want you to have it because even if you don't think you need it today, trust me… you will!

So get access today before the price returns to normal:

[LINK TO SALESPAGE]

...you'll be glad you did. :)

Talk soon,

[YOUR NAME]

*****

Message #: 2

* * * * *

Subj: *[RESULT] For Only $[XX]?*

The fact is, [ISSUE RELATED TO REASON THEY NEED TRAINING/PRODUCT TOPIC].

…any tons of people are panicking about [TOPIC ISSUE].

So you have 2 options:

1. Continue to freak out

OR

2. Check out our new [PROOF RELATED TO TRAINING/PRODUCT] where we show you exactly how we got [RESULT FROM USING TRAINING/ PRODUCT] for only $[XX].

[LINK TO SALESPAGE]

WARNING: Do NOT attempt [ACTION RELATED TO TRAINING/PRODUCT] until you read this.

The fact is, we already [EXPERIENCE RELATED TO TOPIC], so we've already figured out [RESULT].

So, you can try to figure this out on your own…

…or you can get this right now for [X]% off!

[LINK TO SALESPAGE]

Talk soon,

[YOUR NAME]

P.S. The [X]% sale ends [TOMORROW] at [TIME]... please don't pay full price...

Claim your discount here:

[LINK TO SALESPAGE]

*****

Message #: 3

*****

Subj: *[LAST CHANCE] [XX]% off sale ends today!*

A few days ago I released "[NAME OF PRODUCT/ TRAINING]"...

...did you see it?

[LINK TO SALESPAGE]

If not, you need to get yours TODAY because tomorrow the price will be MUCH higher.

So if you're frustrated by [LIST FRUSTRATION], then you need this:

[LINK TO SALESPAGE]

But do it NOW because the [XX]% off flash sale ends [TIME].

Talk soon,

[YOUR NAME]

So there you have it...five different methods for segmenting your list, and two complete campaigns. So now you have ZERO excuses. If you have a list, you can run a Segmentation Campaign. Do it, and watch your unsubscribes plummet while your engagement rates and sales skyrocket.

But what about those subscribers that never engage? What about the leads that join your list, but stop opening or clicking on your messages? What do you do with them? Read on, because that's exactly what we'll be addressing in the next chapter...

Chapter 9:

Phase 5 – Re-Engagement

You're being watched...

Each time you send an email, the "powers that be" judge you. The Internet service providers (ISPs) determine if you're a good guy or a bad guy. The "good guys" get through to the inbox—the "bad guys" get put in the "Spam" folder, or blocked completely.

In a minute you'll learn a simple technique you can use to make sure the ISPs know you are one of the good guys. But first, you need to understand the major variables they consider when determining your fate.

The Big 5 Factors of Email Deliverability

It all boils down to one word... ENGAGEMENT.

The more engaged your email subscribers, the easier it is to get through to the inbox. Makes sense, right? If your email subscribers are engaged you are not likely to be a spammer. The majority of this "Engagement Score" is measured on these five factors:

- Open Rate

- Click Rate

- Share/Forward Rate

- Bounce Rate

- Unsubscribe/Complaint Rate

Notice these are all "rates"—I'll get to why this is important when I outline the actions you must take to increase deliverability. Also, note that the first three rates are positive engagement signals while the fourth and fifth rates are negative signals.

So, the way to greater email deliverability is clear—increase positive engagement rate signals and decrease the negative ones.

Here's how to get it done...

How to Improve Email Engagement Rates

I mentioned that it's important to note that these are rates and not raw numbers. For example, you send an email to a list of 100,000 subscribers with 30,000 opens. That's a 30% open rate—which is respectable. Unfortunately, that still means 70% of your list didn't open the email. Zero engagement. Worse yet, some percentage of those "unopens" will never open an email from you again.

So why should you care?

After all, a 30% open rate is pretty good...why not just let sleeping dogs lie? And who knows, maybe some of those "unopeners" will one day wake up and start engaging with your emails.

Here's the problem with that theory: All those disengaged subscribers—the ones NOT opening and NOT clicking—are hurting your "rates." They're causing your open rates and click-through rates to be lower than they should, and they're also the ones most likely to unsubscribe and complain. And over time, these "low rates" can hurt your deliverability for your entire list...

...meaning your most engaged subscribers may not receive all your emails.

So that's why you should care.

That's why you must be proactive.

And that's why you must perform list hygiene.

The Re-Engagement Phase of the Invisible Selling Machine is more about ensuring you are able to reach your most engaged subscribers—by either reenergizing or removing those with zero engagement. Here's how it works…

Create a Re-Engagement Email Series

First, open your email program and export all your subscribers who haven't opened or clicked an email in the last 60 days. (Most email solutions have this feature built-in. If yours does not, contact customer support and they should be able to walk you through the process manually.)

Next, write up an email series with the goal of re-engaging those disengaged subscribers and moving the into a relevant Engagement Series. Use a subject line like "Are you ok?" or "Is everything ok?" and lead off with something like…

```
Hey… It's been a while since you've opened or
clicked on one of my emails, so I thought I'd
check in on you and let you know what you've
"missed" in the last two months.
```

Include a list of links to content and resources they've been missing. Hit them over the head with the benefit you provide to your email subscribers, and encourage them to opt in to receive a "free gift" of some sort. (By the way, this "free gift" should be a Lead Magnet that places the subscriber in an Engagement Series.)

But don't stop there. Move subscribers that respond (i.e. open and/ or click) out of this Re-Engagement Series, but continue to send the campaign to the remaining disengaged subscribers. You can…

- Inquire whether you have their best email address

- Ask how you can best serve them (i.e. run a survey)

- Offer them a different free gift (i.e. a different Lead Magnet)

- Suggest they read a blog post or watch a video (i.e. a blog launch)

In other words, just hit them with as much content and value as you can for 5 – 7 days. If they still don't respond, it's time to switch gears and start talking about LOSS instead of GAIN...

In the latter stages of this email series, start warning them that you will have to remove them from the list if they don't respond by clicking on a link. Use a subject line like "Should I unsubscribe you?" and lead off with something like...

```
I don't want to keep bothering you with
emails, but I don't want to completely cut
you off, either...
```

But "cut them off" is exactly what you'll do if they do not engage after 3 – 5 emails like these. In the end, you don't have to delete them...simply remove them from your main broadcast list. In fact, I recommend moving these disengaged subscribers into a completely different email service provider just to make sure they can't possibly impact the deliverability of your core list.

You can continue to send this disengaged list affiliate offers or promote a new flagship offer or Lead Magnet, but for the most part, this list is dead. I know that hurts. I know you won't want to remove them. Removing email subscribers you've spent time and money to acquire is never fun, but it is essential to the overall health of your list.

By cutting these lost subscribers, you'll improve your percentage (rate) of opens, clicks and forwards (i.e. good guy signals) and reduce the percentage of bounces, unsubscribes and spam complaints (i.e. bad guy signals). In other words, by taking action to remove these lost subscribers, you've increased your email deliverability, which will only make your "Invisible Selling Machine" more effective and efficient over time.

Once you have a finished "Re-Engagement Campaign" in place, your "Invisible Selling Machine" is built and ready to be deployed. But don't stop there! Your final task is to optimize your "Machine"...

SECTION 3:

Optimizing Your Invisible Selling Machine

Chapter 10:

How To Craft Emails That Convert

Get this right and you'll see increases in...

- Email open rates

- Email click rates, and even...

- Landing page conversion rates

I'm about to share a method for writing high-converting emails by focusing on the "job responsibilities" of each element in that email.

Those elements are...

- The subject line

- The body copy

- The landing page

Each element of your email has a single job, and the smart email marketer employs each element to do its singular job. The frustrated email marketer uses the elements to perform multiple jobs or, even worse, the wrong job. Let's take a look at each element of a single email and the role it plays in the Invisible Selling Machine.

The Role of the Email Subject Line

The subject line has one job and one job alone—to sell the OPEN. Don't try to use the subject line to sell the click, the opt in, or a product. That is not the function of the subject line. There are two main types of subject lines...

- **Blind** - A curiosity based subject line intended to maximize open rate.

- **Direct** - A benefit based subject line that qualifies the reader before opening.

Consider this curiosity-based subject line from the ride-sharing service, Uber...

SUBJ: *Because everyone loves ice cream*

Blind subject lines like this one almost always increase open rates. But, there's a downside. While the open rate will increase, the click rate and/or the conversion rate on the landing page will often decrease.

The reason? The subscriber opening the email is not pre-qualified by the subject line. At some point, either in the email body copy or on the landing page you'll begin to reveal the offer, and a larger percentage of those that opened up because they were curious will find the offer irrelevant, so they'll be out.

But that's not necessarily a bad thing!

If your offer is strong and you know people like it, then volume is the name of the game, and a blind subject line will typically drive more volume than a direct subject line.

Consider the difference between the curiosity based Uber subject line and this one from the personal finance application Mint.com...

SUBJ: *You've been selected to invest with Motif - grow your savings today*

This benefit-driven (direct) subject line qualifies the subscriber.

If they're not interested in growing their savings… they don't open. But a higher percentage of those that do open are more likely to click and convert.

The subject line pre-qualifies them.

Which is better?

Should you use curiosity or direct benefit in your subject lines? The answer: mix it up...but watch your metrics. Monitor...

- opens

- clicks

- and conversions

...by subject line.

But don't stop there—aggressive, curiosity-based subject lines can leave some subscribers with a bad taste in their mouth. If you cross that line, you'll see a greater amount of unsubscribes and complaints on your emails. So, remember, always track and monitor your metrics, and adjust your strategy accordingly.

Now that you know the role of your subject line, let's look at...

The Role of Email Body Copy

The body copy has one job—sell the CLICK.

Just like the subject line you can choose to use curiosity or direct benefit in your email body copy. The same rules apply—curiosity based email copy will increase your click-through rate, but will often decrease your conversion rate on the landing page.

Take a look at this curiosity based email body copy from our company in the survival and preparedness market, SurvivalLife.com…

Subj: *Urgent, this is NOT a Test*

The Emergency Broadcast logo flashed up on your TV screen. You try to click off but it's on every channel...

You start to realize... this is not a test.

A news anchor comes on screen and in a shaky voice says...

"At 9:15 this morning, the U.S. Dollar Collapsed... I repeat the Dollar has Collapsed."

The entire infrastructure of America is now a prime target of opportunity for ANY terrorist attack.

The T.V. suddenly shuts off, moments later, your entire neighborhood goes dark.

You're going to be OK though. This the moment you've prepared for... Right?

[LINK TO SALES PAGE]

Remember, we're all in this together!
'Above Average' Joe

Notice that the subject line is blind and, for the most part, so is the body copy. This message also uses a story to create curiosity—it never directly states the benefit of clicking on the link.

Balance that against the clear benefit laid out in this webinar sign-up email from the analytics software company KISSmetrics...

Subj: *Last Chance to Register: Hooked: How to Build Habit-Forming Products*

[WEBINAR DATE/TIME INFORMATION]

> Nir Eyal, the author of Hooked: How to Build Habit-Forming Products, has constructed a practical framework for designing better products. The framework gives product managers, designers and marketers a new way of thinking of the necessary components of changing user behavior.
>
> Nir will share the tactics companies like Facebook, Pinterest, Instagram, WhatsApp, and Twitter use to drive engagement.

The email then proceeds to lay out exactly what will be learned on the webinar and provides a call to action to register for the webinar.

Very direct.

The benefits of taking action on this email (registering for the webinar) are directly outlined in the email. This pre-qualifies the subscriber and will likely enjoy a higher conversion rate on the registration page (but a lower click through rate) than if they had employed curiosity in the body copy.

Email Body Copy Structure

Unless you're writing a quick, punchy 1 - 2 sentence email, include at least three links to the landing page in your email body copy.

But here's the critical thing…

Whenever possible, each link in the email should provide the reader a different psychological reason to click. Those reasons, in order of appearance, are…

- Curiosity
- Direct benefit
- Scarcity

Take a look at this email copy we sent promoting an offer...

> Subj: *23,247 leads in less than 30 days*
>
> WARNING: Do NOT attempt to run traffic on Facebook until you read this:
>
> [LINK 1 - USING CURIOSITY]
>
> The fact is, we generated 23,247 leads in less than 30 days, so we've already figured out how to drive targeted Facebook traffic and build our lists using social media.
>
> So, you can try to figure this out on your own...
>
> ...or you can get this guide right now [LINK 2 - USING DIRECT BENEFIT] for 85% off.
>
> Talk soon,
> Ryan Deiss
>
> P.S. The 85% sale ends tomorrow at MIDNIGHT... so don't pay full price.
>
> Claim your discount here...
>
> [LINK 3 - USING SCARCITY]

Notice the change in reasoning from one link to the next.

After all, why use curiosity in the second link when it didn't get the click in the first link? Why try another benefit in the 3rd link when it didn't work in the 2nd link?

Mix it up and watch your click through rates soar.

Ok, we know the role of the subject line and body copy but what about...

The Role of the Landing Page

The subject line did its job—it got the OPEN.

The body copy did its job—it got the CLICK.

The role of the landing page is to sell the OPT IN or SALE.

While the landing page is not technically a component of the email—it's critical to understand that neither the subject line nor the email body copy can do the job of the landing page.

We'll get into much more detail about the role of landing pages later in this book but one big idea I wanted to cover as it pertains to the flow of your email marketing is to...

Maintain "Scent"

From subject line to email body copy to landing page your marketing should "smell" the same. In other words, your marketing should remain congruent.

The design should "smell" the same.

The benefits should "smell" the same.

The offer should "smell" the same.

When the "scent" of your marketing breaks from subject line to body copy to landing page—conversion suffers.

Let's take a look at a campaign that uses...

- A direct, benefit-driven subject line

- Direct, benefit-driven body copy

I want you to pay attention to the way the message remains congruent from subject line to body copy to landing page.

Here's the subject line...

Now, notice how the body copy remains congruent with the subject line…

Want to know what the perfect product to sell on Amazon is?

Then download this Checklist now:

No, this checklist won't select the product for you…

…but it's got 22 different criteria to make sure you know if you've got a cash cow or a total "dud" before you ever spend a dime.

And I know it works, because it's the EXACT checklist my friend Ezra uses to select the products he's been selling on Amazon that have **made him MULTIPLE 7-figures in product sales.**

Download your Market Criteria Checklist right now: http://go.digitalmarketer.com/market-criteria-checklist

On the landing page, the design is perfectly congruent with the email...it even uses the exact same image. But the "scent" doesn't stop there. Precisely the same offer that was made in the email is made on the landing page. And the benefits stated on the landing page are reworded and expanded versions of the benefits outlined in the email...

This may seem like common sense... but it certainly isn't common practice. So next time you sit down to write an email—focus on the roles and responsibilities of each component of that email and maintaining "scent" from subject line to body copy to landing page.

Your conversion rate depends on it.

Chapter 11:

My 100 Best Email Subject Line Templates

We send email to millions of people every week, so I've learned a thing or two about writing email subject lines that get opened.

Our best 100 email subject lines are all yours in just a second...

... but first let's look at the elements that make these email subject lines successful.

We talked about Direct Benefit and Curiosity based (Blind) subject lines and body copy in great detail in the Invisible Selling Machine. We also discussed the use scarcity in many of the campaigns.

But there are other characteristics that can get a reader to open up an email. Each of my Top 100 email subject lines contains at least one of these 7 elements:

1 – Direct Benefit

The most straight-forward and clear method for writing an email subject line is to communicate how opening the email will benefit the reader.

How will the content of your email get them something they want? Or, how will it protect them against something they don't want?

2 – Curiosity

A well-crafted curiosity based email subject line will often get outstanding open rates. That said, a curiosity based email subject line, alone, will often fail miserably, so where possible, combine one of these other elements (particularly News or Self Interest) with curiosity.

3 – Scarcity

A powerful element to add to any email subject line is a legitimate reason to act NOW. The best way to move someone to action is to communicate that the resource you're promising in the email is finite in some way.

Can you use, for example, deadlines, limited quantities or seating limitations to communicate urgency or scarcity in your email subject line?

4 – News

You can pull great open rates by communicating that your email contains something that is new to the reader.

5 – Social Proof

People make decisions, in part, by observing the decisions other people have made. Effective email subject lines often provide proof that other people have made the choice you would like your reader to make.

Have an impressive number of people already made the choice you'd like your reader to make?

6 – Story

An email subject line that tells the beginning of a story can be effective. The subject line will need to create curiosity to get opened.

How can your email be wrapped in a story?

7 – Humanity

In the end... people do business with people. Remember to mix some humanity in with your promotional and content email.

How can you connect person to person with your reader?

But don't do this...

Perhaps more importantly—NONE of our best email subject lines are:

- Cute

- Clever

Ok... almost none of our best are cute or clever. Every once in a great while a cute or clever subject line will work...most of the time they will get low open rates.

For the most part it pays to be direct and clear.

Ok...let's take a look at our top email subject lines.

NOTE: The subject lines in this chapter should be used as models for crafting your own subject lines, and shouldn't be copied word-for-word. You are also encouraged to reword them in your "voice," because at the end of the day it's the structure that matters...not the exact words or phrases.

We begin with the 10th best email subject line...

10. Breaking News...

- **Product Type**: Webinar

- **Analysis**: This subject line promises that the reader will find something timely and unknown if they open up.

9. Facebook traffic is dead?

- **Product Type**: Course/Information Product

- **Analysis**: This subject line creates plays on a reader's self interest — particularly those that are using or are considering using Facebook for business.

8. Everybody's waiting for you...

- **Product Type**: Webinar

- **Analysis**: This is a clever way to use urgency in an email subject line. This email was sent a couple of minutes after we started the webinar it was promoting.

7. Kindle bestseller in 4 days?

- **Product Type**: Course/Information Product

- **Analysis**: This subject line promises a benefit in a short amount of time—a good example of a self-interest subject line.

6. Watch live? From anywhere?

- **Product Type**: Event

- **Analysis**: This subject line creates curiosity. It creates the following question in the reader's mind: "Watch what from anywhere?"

5. Facebook closing down?

- **Product Type**: Course/Information Product

- **Analysis**: This is a curiosity subject line that implies that something of self-interest to the reader might be going away.

4. I feel kinda sorry for you...

- **Product Type**: Course/Information Product

- **Analysis**: This subject line plays on the reader's ego and creates curiosity.

3. How to scale your business

- **Product Type**: Service

- **Analysis**: This is a clear and direct self-interest subject-line.

2 . Good news for people who love bad news...

- **Product Type**: Event

- **Analysis**: This one creates curiosity through a cute and clever use of word play.

1. Can't Make The Trip?

- **Product Type**: Event

- **Analysis**: This curiosity subject line asks a question

Ok... that's the Top 10. But there's more... here are the next 90 email subject lines that enjoyed the highest open rates.

- **Your funnel is broken...** – Self Interest

- **[New Video] 1,000,000 customers in 11 months? We have proof.** – News | Self Interest

- **Need my help?** – Self Interest | Curiosity

- **Ahhh, San Diego! Spanish for...** – Curiosity

- **I LOVE this little Facebook tool!** – Self Interest

- **[URGENT] Emergency Gmail Webinar Tomorrow, 7/24!** Urgency | News

- **The Story of "The Vagabonds"** – Story | Curiosity

- **My favorite market research tool** – Self Interest

- **Get your business funded in 2014 [Case Study]** – News | Self Interest

- **Copy & paste this $10 million business...** – Self Interest

- **(time sensitive) Last night's Funnel training...** – Urgency

- **The Ultimate Facebook "Cheat Sheet"** – Self Interest

- **Create your own digital magazine (no iPhone/iPad required)** – Self Interest

- **Will this KILL your business in 2014?** – Curiosity | News | Self Interest

- **Questions about War Room?** – Self Interest

- **[TONIGHT] My proven funnel system revealed...** – Urgency | Self Interest

- **[Last Chance] Create the perfect funnel...** – Urgency | Self Interest

- **[PROOF] How to get 10 cent email leads from Facebook...** – Self Interest

- **[Free Book] The $10 million discovery (limited)** – Self Interest | News | Scarcity

- **Boost your email click-throughs by 200%** – Self Interest

- **No more discounts on T&C!** – Self Interest | Scarcity

- **Facebook sucks** – Curiosity

- **[FLASH SALE] This is how we get traffic from Amazon** – Urgency | Self Interest

- **[Open NOW] The Digital Publishing Blueprint is LIVE!** – News | Self Interest

- **The Perfect Webinar Funnel** – Self Interest

- **Tim Ferriss says "Hi"** – Social Proof

- **Pulling FBAdpower DOWN...** – Scarcity

- **LAST CHANCE for Livestreaming...** – Urgency

- **New site and new sales in 3 days or less?!** – Self Interest

- **1 cent CLICKS?! (open up)...** – Self Interest | Curiosity

- **I hope they're not mad...** – Curiosity

- **[Closing Tomorrow] Don't get shut out... again!** – Urgency

- **Good News... Your 1st sale in 3 days...** – Self Interest

- **How I get dirt-cheap, high-quality traffic...** – Self Interest

- **[FINAL PLAYING] Emergency Gmail Webinar!** – Urgency | News

- **Will 2014 be better than 2013?** – Curiosity | News

- **T&C CLOSING! Only 61 spots left!** – Scarcity

- **Facebook "panic" is great news for you...** – News | Self Interest

- **[CLOSING TONIGHT] T&C tickets GONE tonight...** – Scarcity

- **[JUST RELEASED] More T&C Tickets Available...** – News | Urgency

- **Software cherry-picks the hottest leads for you...** – Self Interest

- **Free 68 page book Interview With A Mega-Bestseller** – Self Interest

- **[FLASH SALE] Get targeted FB leads for dirt cheap...** – Urgency | Self Interest

- **[Finally] Get this Proven Digital Marketing Blueprint** – Self Interest | News

- **85% sale ends today** – Urgency

- **You an Amazon Bestseller?** – Self Interest

- **Last chance – T&C Closing at Midnight TONIGHT!** – Urgency

- **Important letter for you** – Curiosity

- **[NEWS] EmailWorld 2013 Sept. 24th and 25th in San Diego, CA** – News

- **Announced 306% increase in FB traffic?** – News | Self Interest

- **Facebook OWNS Google...** – Curiosity

- **[Almost Gone] New T&C Tickets going fast...** – Scarcity

- **[IMPORTANT] Gmail Webinar TODAY!** – Urgency

- **Only open if your business will do at least 7-figures this year...** – Curiosity | Self Interest

- **Apple Newsstand training is CLOSING** – Urgency

- **FW: Did you miss this yesterday?** – Curiosity

- **Merry Christmas to You!** – Humanity

- **Can I help you build your sales funnel?** – Self Interest

- **"Panda" update for Facebook?** – Curiosity | News

- **Press Releases More Powerful Than Ever?** – News | Curiosity

- **Last chance for Apple Newsstand training [FREE RESOURCE]** – Urgency | Self Interest

- **Interact with the industry's brightest minds at the QuickSprout Forum** – Self Interest

- **You on Facebook?** – Curiosity

- **Turn Ideas into Million-Dollar Products** – Self Interest

- **100,000 unique visitors PER MONTH...** – Self Interest

- **The "Mystery Man" Behind 500 Product Launches...** – Curiosity | News

- **This 1 "weird trick" is worth the trip** – Curiosity | Self Interest

- **Arrested for printing money?** – Curiosity | News

- **Can we meet in San Diego?** – Curiosity | Self Interest

- **Bad news and good news...** – Curiosity | News

- **T&C is selling out! Only 32 seats left!** - Scarcity

- **Ex-construction worker earns $309/day with...** – Story | News

- **This Free book changed my business...** – Curiosity | Self Interest

- **The free books are all gone...** – Curiosity | Scarcity

- **[NEWS] 5th Annual Traffic & Conversion Summit OPEN** – News

- **[80% Discount] Game-changing software...** – Self Interest

- **Content idea generator [Free Resource 1 of 3]** – Self Interest

- **[RESULTS] My Facebook Case Study** – Self Interest | News

- **THIS Increased Conversions 24%?!?** – Self Interest | News

- **FINAL NOTICE: Only 11 seats left!** – Scarcity

- **Only 187 free copies of Frank's book left...** – Scarcity

- **No list & NO partners = sales in 3 days?!** – Self Interest | Curiosity

- **Your "On Demand" bootcamp replay...** – Self Interest

- **Happy Thanksgiving!** – Humanity

- **How I "busted-up" Google's monopoly...** – Curiosity | News

- **[SPOOKY NOTICE] 82% off T&C Tickets (CLOSING 24 hours)** – Urgency

- **Your DEADline is tonight! 82% off dies at midnight...** – Urgency

- **If I had to start all over again...** – Story

- **Wanna pick an $80 Million brain...** – Curiosity | Self Interest

- **[REVEALED] Turn Likes into email subscribers fast...** – News | Self Interest

Chapter 12:

8-Point Lead Magnet Checklist

This little baby generated 28,507 leads in 45 days...

It's called a Lead Magnet and if you don't have one—or don't have a good one—this one aspect of the Invisible Selling Machine could literally change your life.

Lead Magnets are used to generate brand new leads, but they're also used to move existing leads from the Segmentation Phase of the Invisible Selling Machine into the Value Loop created by the Engagement and Ascension Phases. And the better your Lead Magnet, the more leads you'll have in your Engagement and Ascension Series. (And remember...that's where the money is made.)

We're going to look at 9 different types of Lead Magnets in this section and review a checklist you'll use to create Lead Magnets that perform well in your Invisible Selling Machine.

Before we look at the types of Lead Magnets, you need a quick taste of the success factors we'll cover later in the Lead Magnet Checklist. First, you need to understand the single most important element of a successful Lead Magnet...

Specificity

I have great news.

Lead Magnets don't have to be lengthy. Or complex. Or time-intensive to create. In fact, a long and complex Lead Magnet will likely convert poorly. You simply need to solve a <u>specific</u> problem with a solution for a <u>specific</u> segment of your market.

Here's the key: Your Lead Magnet must be consumed by the prospect for it to have an impact. The perfect Lead Magnet will offer tremendous value within 5 minutes of the opt in. This is a "rule of thumb", of course, but we don't recommend, for example, a mini-course delivered over 14 days or a 300-page eBook as a Lead Magnet. These Lead Magnets take too long to consume and are unlikely to be specific.

Notice how simple and specific this Lead Magnet is...

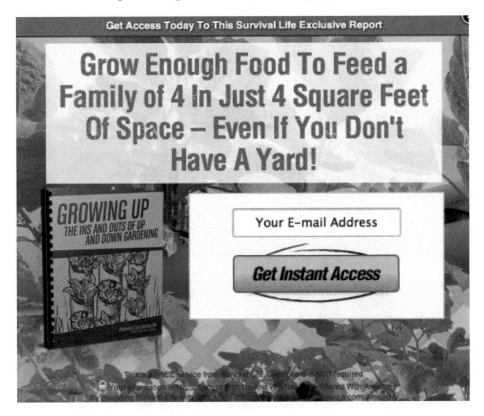

On the other hand, this Lead Magnet is non-specific and takes 20-weeks to receive the full pay off...

Shoot for the former and not the latter when creating your Lead Magnets. The good news is that the first one is much easier to create than the second one—and it will convert better.

Types of Lead Magnets

We'll take a deeper dive into the factors that determine the success of your Lead Magnet in just a minute. First, let's look at some Lead Magnet types (with examples) that do it right...

1 – Case Studies

A case study is my favorite type of Lead Magnet because it's a naturally specific type of content. Case Studies also fit easily into a number of the other criteria we'll cover later in the Lead Magnet Checklist.

This video is a simple screencast using software like Camtasia or Screenflow that we used to deliver a case study at Digital Marketer.

This first video delivered the first part of the case study and made a pitch to receive the second part if an email address is entered.

2 – Guide/Report

Reports and Guides are amongst the most common types of Lead Magnets. If you use a Lead Magnet of this type—be careful. You could easily violate the specificity rule. Here's an example Free Report Lead Magnet opt in from my friend Joe Polish at Piranha Marketing.

Notice that Joe isn't promising to change your life or make all your wildest dreams come true. He's simply showing you a 7-step process for writing a successful ad...something he knows will appeal to his target market.

3 – Cheat Sheet/Handout

Cheat sheets and handouts make excellent Lead Magnets. They have a different "feel" to them than Reports or Guides, because they are generally very short (one page or so) and cut straight to an ultra-specific point. You can deliver these as checklists, mind maps or "blueprints."

Here's an example mind map used as a Lead Magnet...

Notice how the mind map is blurred out to build curiosity.

In one case, we actually used a NAPKIN (or the image of it) as a Lead Magnet, and to date it's one of our most effective campaigns...

"Written On This Ordinary, Everyday Cocktail Napkin Is A Business Model That Has Literally Made Me MILLIONS of Dollars Online. **Now I Want To Give It To You...For FREE!**"

My name is Ryan Deiss and I want to give you my entire online marketing business model...the exact same business model that has allowed me to make many millions of dollars online in just a few short years.

It's not complicated...

In fact, the entire business model fits on a single napkin. (That's what I wrote it on when I first conceived this model back in September of 2006.)

Just enter your email address in the form to the right, and I'll send you:

- A PDF copy of my handwritten "Million Dollar Napkin" business plan...

Free Instant Access Instructions:

Enter your email address in the form below for instant access to the "Million Dollar Napkin" business model plus 3 bonus training videos not available anywhere else...

Enter Your Email: [   ]

[Free Instant Access!]

4 – Toolkit/Resource List

A Toolkit or Resource List can make a great Lead Magnet for the right business and market. This company is offering a Time Management Toolkit in exchange for contact information...

...and this is one of the tools that is delivered after the Lead Magnet is taken by the prospective lead:

As you can see, it isn't a lengthy report or video. It's just a simple spreadsheet that anyone interested in time management will find valuable.

5 – Software Download/Free Trial

Software companies often offer a Free Trial of their software as a Lead Magnet. Here's how Bidsketch, a SAAS proposal building application, asks for an opt in to start a free trial...

Shopify.com is even more sophisticated with their trial offer Lead Magnets. As an ecommerce store builder, they have a number of different features and can build many different types of stores. But rather than highlight all their features when asking for a trial, they instead create multiple Lead Magnets...one for each feature.

For example, here's a Shopify trial page offering a "Facebook Store" as a Lead Magnet:

SOURCE: http://www.shopify.com/facebook

...and here's another one offering a "WordPress Store"...

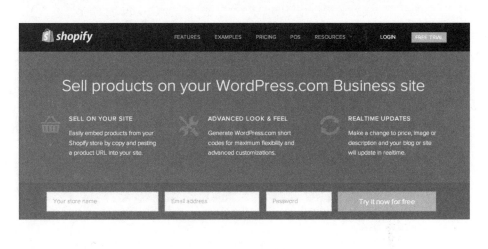

Getting started is easy

Embed products on your WordPress.com site in three quick steps.

Install the WordPress.com app

Sign up for your Shopify store, upload your products, and install the WordPress.com app from the Shopify App Store.

Activate the Shopify plugin

Activate the Shopify ecommerce plugin in your Wordpress.com dashboard and type in your Shopify store URL.

Manage your payments

Within your Shopify admin, select one of our 70+ payment gateway and start accepting orders from your blog or site.

SOURCE: http://www.shopify.com/wordpress

In both cases, the user is actually signing up for a complete trial to Shopify, but by creating multiple, SPECIFIC Lead Magnets, they are able to appeal to different user subsets which increases conversions.

6 – Discount/Free Shipping

For those selling physical products on or off-line, discount clubs or Free Shipping offers can be an effective Lead Magnet type. Here's how NewEgg generates new leads using an offer of Promo Codes sent to the email inbox. (See the bar at the very top of the page and down at the bottom of the page.)

7 – Quiz/Survey

Quizzes and surveys can be a very engaging way to generate new leads, because participants will opt in just to receive the results. The only downside to this type of lead magnet is they can be more complex to build. Fortunately, there are tools on the market such as Interact (see: http://www.TryInteract.com) that you can use to create quizzes even if you aren't a programmer.

Here's an example of a quiz being used by a home improvement company...

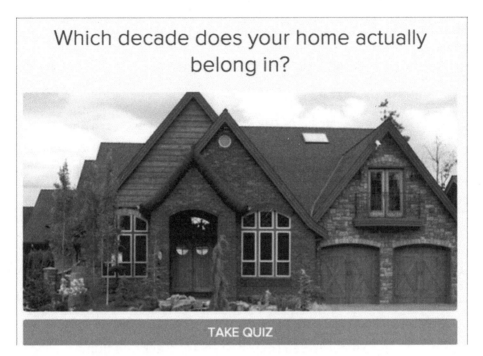

After clicking the "Take Quiz" button, the following questions are displayed. (Notice how they're having fun and displaying a little personality in the answer choices. Very smart.)

> ## Which best describes your homes energy efficiency?
>
> ☐ The Flintstone Car
>
> ☐ The Little Engine That Could
>
> ☐ Tree Huggers
>
> ☐ Beam Me Up Scotty

Once all the questions are answered, the prospect is presented with this opt in form...

Simple! They register to see their results (and get free home improvement tips), and the site owner has a fresh lead they can add to an Engagement Series.

8 – Assessment/Test

An assessment or test can make a powerful Lead Magnet, particularly if it is delivered online to increase the speed of consumption and gratification. HubSpot, a company that sells marketing software, has been generating leads with their "Marketing Grader" for years...

These assessments require a fair bit of custom programming and design to implement, but when deployed properly they're one of the most effective Lead Magnet types of all.

9 – Sales Material

It may sound crazy, but in some cases, the most desired piece of information for the market is pricing and descriptions of products or services. Ikea harvests contact information in exchange for their catalog, and they can deliver it digitally to speed up consumption and gratification.

Now that you understand the different types of Lead Magnets, let's talk about how you can optimize them to improve conversion rates and lead-flow...

8-Point Lead Magnet Checklist

The purpose of a Lead Magnet is to provide an irresistible bribe that compels your market to give you their contact information. But all Lead Magnets are not created equal, so over the years I've developed a checklist to evaluate the effectiveness of a given offer.

Run your Lead Magnet offer through this checklist. The more checkmarks, the better your Lead Magnet will perform:

- Offers an ultra-specific solution to an ultra-specific market

- Promises "one big thing" (as opposed to a lot of little things)

- Speaks to a known desired end result (Shows Interest/Intent)

- Offers immediate gratification (no newsletters, podcasts, etc.)

- Moves prospect down a "continuum of belief" – They might believe in you (if you have proof) but they don't think THEY can do it

- Has a high perceived value

- Has a high ACTUAL value

- Rapidly Consumable (No books, 30 day courses, etc.)

Let's take a look at each of these Lead Magnet success factors in detail...

1. Offers an Ultra-Specific Solution

Lead magnets should NEVER be vague. They must offer an ultra-specific solution to an ultra-specific market. This is the #1 problem with most Lead Magnets—they simply aren't specific enough.

If you focus on being specific, you'll find that most of the next 7 factors on this checklist will take care of themselves...

2. Promises "One Big Thing"

Your prospects want the "silver bullet," so it's always better to make and deliver one big promise as opposed to a lot of little ones. If you have a book or a 12-week course or a 50-page report—look for the "One Big Thing" that will really move the needle for that specific segment of the market. That's your Lead Magnet!

And here's the great news: If you were about to sit down and crank out a book to give away as a Lead Magnet—you can stop. It's not necessary and, in fact, our testing shows time and time again that finding the "One Big Thing" and delivering that will outperform that book, long-form white paper or 50-page report every day of the week.

3. Speaks to a Known Desired End Result

What does your market REALLY want? If you can figure that out and offer a Lead Magnet that promises it, they'll gladly give you their contact information.

Consider a Lead Magnet titled, *"The Plumbers Guide to Internet Marketing"*

While this Lead Magnet has it half right (it speaks to a specific segment of the market) it does not speak to the desired end result of the plumber.

Plumbers don't want to learn Internet marketing. They want the phone to ring. They want more customers. This Lead Magnet will perform poorly because it doesn't tap into the prospect's actual desires.

Lastly, when you speak to a specific end result with your Lead Magnet, the act of opting in indicates interest in the topic of that Lead Magnet, which should trigger a new Engagement Series dedicated to that topic. In other words, the Lead Magnet is the entry-point to your Invisible Selling Machine, but that only works if your lead magnet is SPECIFIC and topical. (NOTE: We discussed this concept back in chapter 6, but it's important enough that it bears repeating.)

So for example, imagine you have three products in the golf niche, each of which appeals to a different desired end result:

- **Product 1** - Improves your drive

- **Product 2** - Improves your "short game"

- **Product 3** - Improves your putting

Each of these flagship products should have at least one Lead Magnet that speaks to the end result provided by each product. So if a subscriber opts in to receive a Lead Magnet about improving their putting, then they have expressed interest in improving their putting game and are therefore a perfect candidate for an Engagement Series that sells Product 3. In other words...

The *topic* of the Lead Magnet informs the *topic* of the Engagement series, which should lead to the sale of a *topical* product. Make sense?

4. Offers Immediate Gratification

Your market wants a solution and they want it NOW. And that's why your Lead Magnet will perform better if your prospects know they can get the "One Big Thing" we discussed earlier in this checklist—right now.

Avoid using email newsletters, multi-day courses and other resources that fail to deliver the NOW. You can test bundling a newsletter with your ultra-specific, "One Big Thing" but a newsletter on it's own doesn't offer immediate gratification—and it won't perform well as a stand-alone Lead Magnet.

5. Moves Prospect Down a "Continuum of Belief"

If somebody is going to take an action (i.e. opt in, make a purchase, come into your store, etc.) they have to believe they can achieve the end result that is being promised. The big mistake marketers make is they believe that the prospect's primary objection to moving forward is that they don't believe in YOU—the marketer.

That's not the case. The biggest hurdle to overcome is the prospect's lack of belief in THEMSELVES. Sure, you'll need to provide proof that you can be trusted—but that's a far easier objection to overcome.

Don't believe me? Then consider the difficulty of selling a back pain related product or service. Whether you're selling pills, acupuncture or surgery, the problem is the same: The prospect has tried EVERYTHING!

They simply can't imagine a life without back pain, and they're worried that if they give you money they'll simply be disappointed again (but have less cash).

So how do you overcome this problem?

Yes, you need your marketing to show how your solution is different and better than everything they've tried in the past, but what's even more important is to offer a Lead Magnet that allows them to believe that they can some day be pain-free. In other words, you need to offer them a "little victory."

So, if your Lead Magnet shows them a simple stretch that provides temporary relief, that might be enough to make them believe. Even if the stretch doesn't provide long-term relief, it's enough to give them hope. It's enough to help them remember what it felt like to not have back pain. In short, it's enough to move them down the "continuum of belief" so they will be receptive to buy whatever product or service you offer them in your Engagement Series.

Remember this: The best Lead Magnets show the prospect something they didn't know that makes them believe they can finally achieve the result you're promising. If you can deliver this, you'll not only have a higher opt in rate, but you'll improve your sales conversions as well.

6. Has a High Perceived Value

Just because it's free, doesn't mean it should LOOK free. Use professional graphics and imagery to establish real monetary value in the mind of the visitor. And remember, people don't buy products online—they buy pictures of products online. So make sure the picture of Lead Magnet adequately expresses the VALUE of your Lead Magnet.

7. Has a High ACTUAL Value

Hopefully this one goes without saying, but I'm going to say it anyway just to be safe...

If your Lead Magnet is all sizzle and no steak, you may get their contact information, but you'll lose their attention. To win, you must promise AND DELIVER the goods.

8. Rapidly Consumable

You don't want your Lead Magnet to be a roadblock on the path to making a purchase, so ideally it should be consumed or experienced in 5 minutes or less. This is optional, and the "5 Minute Rule" is much more of a guideline than a law. But as we've already discussed, if the Lead Magnet is difficult to consume (i.e. a 300-page book or a 30-day course) the conversion rates on this offer suffer because the prospect will naturally want to consume it before taking further action.

Here's the big takeaway on Lead Magnets...

Many of the items in this checklist boil down to this underlying principle: specificity matters.

Take a look at your Lead Magnet through the eyes of this checklist...

Are you promising too much?

Are you being too vague?

If so, test something more specific.

Finding the Lead Magnet "Hook"

You know your topic better than anyone else, but sometimes that can be a barrier to determining the topic of your Lead Magnet. It's like my mentor, Roy Williams, *The Wizard of Ads*, says: ***"It's impossible to read the label from inside the bottle."***

So here are a couple questions you can ask to help see your business from outside of the bottle. When you're brainstorming Lead Magnet ideas, ask yourself: *"If I had two minutes to impress someone, what would I say, show or give them that would blow their mind?"*

That's your Lead Magnet.

Or, ask this question: *What's the one thing, more than anything else, my prospects truly want to know?*

In the real estate market, it might be: "How much is my property worth?"

In the dating market it might be: "How do I know when she's ready to be kissed?

In the social media marketing space it might be, "How do I run a Facebook contest?"

Answer that question and you've got your Lead Magnet.

Chapter 13:

16-Point Landing Page Checklist

You've got a solid Lead Magnet that's ready to pump fresh leads into your Invisible Selling Machine. Now what?

If your Lead Magnet offer is right, the only thing between you and a steady stream of leads is traffic and a high-converting landing page. We'll get to traffic in just a second... first let's make sure that landing page is ready to convert your new prospects into leads.

When you use good landing page software you're getting access to proven templates that make it easy building landing pages for your Lead Magnet. This, along with ease of use, are the big reasons to use applications like Optimize Press or LeadPages.net to build landing or "squeeze pages."

A squeeze page is a type of landing page that gives the visitor two options:

- Enter your contact information

- Exit

There are no links or other distractions on a squeeze page (aside from links to a Privacy Policy or any other mandatory pages).

For example, remember this Lead Magnet?

The page on which the Lead Magnet is delivered is a squeeze page.

Notice the simplicity of the squeeze page. It includes...

- A headline
- A sub headline
- Benefit Bullets
- The offer
- A call to action
- Social Proof (The "As Seen On" logos)

When the visitor clicks on the "Download Now" button, they are presented with this opt in form...

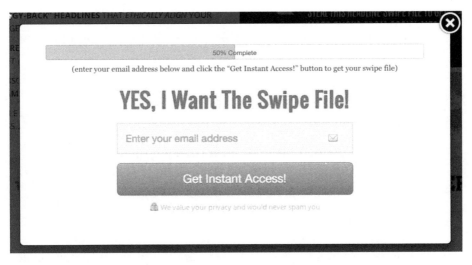

By using simple landing page software to build this squeeze page, new leads are automatically synced to our email system and ready to receive an Engagement Series. I highly recommend using landing page software like LeadPages.net or Optimize Press to create your Lead Magnet squeeze pages.

Use this checklist to build a squeeze page that converts prospects into leads that feed your Invisible Selling Machine.

- **Market Callout** – Your visitor needs to know they're in the right place, so make sure you call out to them either directly (ATTENTION: _____) or indirectly with recognizable images and vocabulary.

- **Clear and Concise** – The best landing pages have a single message and make a single offer. Make sure your landing page isn't trying to do too much.

- **Easily Understood** – If a visitor can't figure out what you're offering in 5 seconds or less, you'll lose them. Perform the 5-second test with friends or colleagues and make sure your landing page passes.

- **Compelling Headline** – You need a clear, concise, benefit-rich headline that grabs your reader's attention and tells them they've come to the right place.

- **CTA Above the Fold** – Most of your visitors won't scroll below the fold, so if you're making a free Lead Magnet offer, give them a chance to take action without scrolling.

- **Contrasting Button Color** – There's a lot of debate about button colors, but one constant is that the button color should contrast (NOT blend in) with the surrounding design elements.

- **Custom Button Text** – "Submit" is not good enough. Test button text that gives a specific command or speaks to the end result. (i.e. "Get Free Instant Access")

- **Social Proof** – "As seen on" logos, testimonials, or referencing the number of downloads/subscribers all let your visitors know they're making a smart decision by opting in to your Lead Magnet.

- **Limited Navigation** – The best landing pages offer only two options: opt in or exit. To maximize conversions, keep navigation to a minimum.

- **Visual Cues** – The landing page should incorporate arrows, boxes and other visual devices to draw the eye to the call to action area.

- **Hero Shot** – Typically an image or graphical representation of the Lead Magnet will bump conversions, but not always. So start with it as a control, but make a note to test without it.

- **Limited Form Fields** – Don't ask for information you don't need! If you only plan to follow-up via email, just ask for name and email, at most. (In fact, test dropping the name field, too, if you don't plan to personalize your follow-up messages.)

- **Source Congruency** – Also called "scent." The text and imagery on the landing page should match (ideally exactly) the text and imagery that was in whatever ad or creative that brought the visitor to the landing page.

- **Brand Consistency** – You don't have to stick your logo on every landing page, but the overall look and feel should be consistent with your core brand.

- **Sharing Enabled** – While landing pages don't typically go viral, some of your more altruistic visitors will click Facebook and Twitter share buttons, so make it easy and obvious for them to do so.

- **Visible Privacy Policy and TOS** – Not only are privacy policies and terms of service required to advertise on some platforms (including Google AdWords) but they're also good for conversions.

So now that we know WHERE we're sending traffic to convert into new leads, it's time to generate some traffic and make some money...

Chapter 14:

Big Traffic...Big List

Alright, it's time to answer the big question...

"Now that I have an 'Invisible Selling Machine,' how do I get traffic and leads?"

It's a good question, because even the most efficient machines can't run without fuel, and traffic is the "fuel" that drives your Invisible Selling Machine.

Fortunately, traffic is all around you. Google, Facebook and LinkedIn have billions of users, and they'll happily send their users to your landing page. You just need to cut them a check.

So traffic is easy.

If you want it, you buy it.

That's it!

Don't believe me? Then consider this...

What if I promised to pay you $10 CASH every time you generated a visitor to your Lead Magnet landing page? Think about it. $10 in your pocket for every single visitor that comes to your landing page. Now do you think you could get traffic to that page? Of course! If you had $10 to spend on every click...*traffic would be easy!*

So there you have it...

You don't actually have a traffic problem.

If you want it, you buy.

The trick is, how can you afford to buy the fuel your machine desperately needs? Fortunately, you're off to a great start...

With the right Lead Magnet in place and the Invisible Selling Machine behind it, you will make sales. The traffic you receive WILL convert into revenue, so you will have the funds to buy more fuel. So that's the good news. And that's why, up until now, traffic was so much more difficult to acquire. Maybe even impossible.

You see, without a "machine" that's capable of converting your traffic into leads and leads into sales, your options are very limited. You either need to raise a bunch of money from investors (so you can buy traffic at a loss) or you need to manipulate the search engines into sending you "free traffic." And neither of those methods are easy...or guaranteed.

But this method...the one you just learned is guaranteed.

You now have the power. You are now able to turn traffic into money. It's as close to alchemy as humans have ever come, and you know how to do it. So as long as you are making more from your traffic than you are spending, the fuel is endless.

Traffic becomes perpetual.

Unfortunately, there is no one way to get traffic. In fact, the actual step-by-step tactics of getting traffic from Facebook and Google change quickly. They change so quickly, in fact, that I would be doing you a disservice if I published them in this book, because by the time it reached your hands, the traffic strategy would surely be outdated.

So here's what I'm going to do for you instead...

I'm not just going to tell you how to get traffic...I'm going to SHOW you how to get traffic. And I'm going to do it for you for free.

Just go to this page, and register for the bonus traffic training:

http://www.followupmachine.com/traffic-bonus

When you do, you'll receive access to the most up-to-date traffic-getting, list-building methods we're currently deploying at DigitalMarketer. And as an added bonus, you'll also see how we deploy our "Invisible Selling Machine," because by registering for this bonus training (i.e. Lead Magnet) you'll also become a subscriber to the DigitalMarketer newsletter, and you'll be placed in a relevant Engagement Series. (In fact, if you're a brand-new subscriber to DigitalMarketer, you'll also receive our Indoctrination Series.)

You can obviously unsubscribe at any time and you'll still be able to access the bonus traffic training. But I don't think you'll want to do that. For one, I truly believe you'll enjoy the content you receive from DigitalMarketer. More importantly, though, I think you'll enjoy "playing customer" and seeing how we deploy the "Invisible Selling Machine" on you.

Is it a little bit sneaky?

Is it a little bit "meta?"

Maybe.

But if you've read this far, I think you'll get a kick out of it, and I know I'll be thrilled to have you as a subscriber. :)

Chapter 15:

Unleash Your Machine

What? You're still reading?

But the book is finished.

Over.

I told you everything...

...or did I? :)

The fact is, the concept of "Invisible Selling" is hard to explain in print alone. That's why, if you would like to see a complete video walk-through of the "Invisible Selling Machine," from yours truly, you can get it now by going to:

http://followupmachine.com/ultimate-email-gameplan

When you register, you'll also receive a graphical flowchart of "The Machine" that you can print and use for note taking. (You may even decide to hang a picture of it by your desk like some of our readers have done.)

But whatever you do, don't stop now!

You already know more than all your competitors combined about email marketing and "invisible selling," but unless you put these concepts into practice they'll do you no good.

So here's a 7-step plan that will get you started:

1. Start writing your Indoctrination Series. It's only 2 or 3 emails, so you should be able to knock it out in a day or two... tops.

2. Then move on to your Engagement Series. Just make sure you're crafting that Engagement Series such that it follows a compelling Lead Magnet, and then ensure that the Lead Magnet funnels into a topically-relevant core product or service. Once your Engagement Series is in place...

3. Start writing an Ascension Series that will convert your new buyers into multi-buyers. With that half of your "Machine" complete...

4. Begin driving leads using the strategies I taught you in the bonus traffic training (see Chapter 14). Once the traffic is flowing, you can then...

5. Start writing Segmentation campaigns for the leads that don't engage or ascend.

6. Your final step is to craft a Re-Engagement Series for the previously engaged leads who slip through the cracks. Now your "machine" is complete, but your work isn't...

7. Continue optimizing your "Invisible Selling Machine" using the checklists I gave you in this section.

That's it!

Your machine is built.

Congratulations!

You now have a business asset that will continue to generate sales for your business effortlessly...

...Perpetually.

...Invisibly.

About the Author

Ryan Deiss is the co-founder of Idea Incubator LP and CEO of DigitalMarketer.com. He launched his first web-based business from his college dorm room in 1999, and since that time he's founded over 40 different businesses (and partnered in dozens more) in markets such as health and beauty, survival and preparedness, DIY crafts and home improvement, investing and finance, chemical and liquid filter manufacturing, business lending, online skills training and menswear...just to name a few.

In fact, over the last 36 months Ryan and his team have:

- Invested over $15,000,000 on marketing tests...

- Generated tens of millions of unique visitors...

- Sent well over a BILLION permission-based emails, and...

- Run approximately 3,000 split and multi-variant tests...

...so he knows a thing or two about marketing and selling online.

In addition to operating multiple businesses, Ryan is also a highly sought after author, speaker and consultant whose work has impacted over 250,000 businesses in 68 different countries.

For more information about Ryan, you can check out his personal page at RyanDeiss.com, or reach out to him on Facebook and Twitter at:

Facebook: http://www.facebook.com/ryandeiss

Twitter: https://www.twitter.com/ryandeiss